NEW YORK STATE
SCIENCE
COACH, GRADE 8

by Elise Russo, Ed.D.

EDI 797

CONTENTS

Part I: SCIENCE REVIEW

3. Standard 4: Science
Part 2—The Physical Setting

Part II: PRACTICE TESTS

To the Student

Every year, New York students in the eighth grade take a series of exams that test how much they have learned in school. One of these is the **Grade 8 Intermediate-Level Science Test**. This book, the **New York Science Coach, Grade 8**, will help you understand the kinds of questions that will be on this test. It will review important concepts in science that you may be tested on. And it will give you practice on questions like the ones on the exam.

What is This Test About?

The test (and this book) concentrates mostly on the concepts and skills found in two areas:

- **Analysis, Inquiry, and Design**—Questions that test your understanding of scientific investigation: how scientists pose questions, look for answers, and develop solutions to scientific and technological problems.

- **Science**—Questions that test your understanding of scientific concepts, principles, and theories concerning the living environment and the physical (nonliving) world.

The test itself is in two parts: a written test, where you answer written questions, and a performance test, where you use scientific equipment to find answers to the questions asked of you.

How Will the Book Help Me?

To help you prepare for the test, the book is divided into three parts:

PART 1. Science Review. This part contains—

- **Example questions** like the ones on the test. There are three kinds:

  —<u>Multiple-choice questions</u>—where you pick the correct answer from the four choices given.

  — <u>Short-answer questions</u>—where you write one or two sentences to answer a question, or where you read a data table, complete a graph, or use some other skill that scientists use in their work.

  —<u>Extended-response questions</u>—where you read a few paragraphs on some science topic and then answer some questions in a short paragraph or two.

- **Discussion sections**, one for each example, that contain—

  —detailed explanations of the correct answers to each question.

  —explanations of why the other answers are not correct.

PART 2. Practice Tests. This part contains two complete, 45-question practice science tests.

- **Practice Test 1** is based on the *Intermediate-Level Practice Test Sampler* distributed by New York. It is followed by detailed explanations of the correct and incorrect answers to each question.
- **Practice Test 2** is a final exam for you to test yourself on.

PART 3. The Performance Test (also called "PART D"). This part contains a brief discussion of some sample tasks for the Performance Test. In that test you will be asked to use some scientific equipment to find answers to the questions asked of you. Equipment you will have used during your science lessons in class will be set up for you and you will go to each area and answer the questions given.

Two Important Suggestions

Here are two suggestions on how to get the most out of this book:

- Try to complete each question. This will make you think about it, even if you don't get the answer right at first.
- The answers to each question can be found in the discussion section that follows the question. *Read the <u>entire</u> discussion after each question, even if you got the answer right!* The discussions contain valuable information on related topics that may appear on the test.

Good Luck on the Test!

To the Teacher

This book, *The New York Science Coach, Grade 8*, is designed to help prepare your students for **New York's Grade 8 Intermediate-Level Science Test**.

In 1996, the New York State Board of Regents adopted *Learning Standards for Mathematics, Science, and Technology*. These Learning Standards tell teachers, administrators, and parents what students should know and be able to do in mathematics, science, and engineering design by the time they graduate from high school.

There are seven learning standards in mathematics, science, and technology. They include:

1. **Analysis, Inquiry, and Design** – where students will pose questions, seek answers, and develop solutions.

2. **Information Systems** – where students will access, generate, process, and transfer information using appropriate technologies.

3. **Mathematics** – where students will communicate and reason mathematically and apply mathematics to real-world settings.

4. **Science** – where students will apply scientific concepts, principles, and theories to the physical setting and the living environment.

5. **Technology** – where students will apply technological knowledge and skills to design, construct, use, and evaluate products and systems to satisfy human and environmental needs.

6. **Interconnectedness: Common Themes** – where students will understand relationships and common themes that connect mathematics, science, and technology and apply these themes to these and other areas of learning.

7. **Interdisciplinary Problem Solving** – where students will apply the knowledge and thinking skills of mathematics, science, and technology to address real-life problems and make informed decisions.

In order to make sure students are learning what they need along the way, they must take several state examinations; one in 4th grade, one in 8th grade, and at least one Regents examination in high school. Some of the standards listed on the previous page will be tested in examinations specific to those areas, such as mathematics and technology (Standards 3 and 5). Other standards can be tested better with projects or other work in your classroom, such as Standards 2, 6, and 7.

The *Intermediate-Level Science Test* concentrates on Standards 1 and 4. It is designed to show your students' progress in reaching the science standards that are important for all students in New York State. These standards were designed to help students learn to think about science concepts in a broad way and be able to apply their knowledge and skills to new situations. It is less important to concentrate on the details and more important to get a bigger picture of how science can help make the world a better place.

The following will serve as a review of the Science Learning Standards that are available for testing on the examination:

List of Standards

The standards include important Key Ideas—concepts that students should be familiar with. The Key Ideas are the same as those in elementary school and high school, but the concepts and skills (called *Performance Indicators*) that students must know are specific to the Intermediate Level and might appear on the *Intermediate-Level Science Test*.

Standard 1. This standard includes seven Key Ideas:

Mathematical Analysis

Key Idea 1—Abstraction and symbolic representation are used to communicate mathematically. Students need to be able to use numbers and other symbols to describe and compare quantities and show mathematical relationships. Students should be able to identify independent and dependent variables and identify relationships among them.

Key Idea 2—Deductive and inductive reasoning are used to reach mathematical conclusions. Students need to be able to use inductive reasoning to reach conclusions. Inductive reasoning allows students to make generalizations about phenomena by interpreting data and examining patterns and relationships.

Key Idea 3—Critical thinking skills are used in the solution of mathematical problems. Students need to be able to apply mathematical knowledge and appropriate scientific tools, including pictures, charts, and tables to solve problems about the natural world.

Scientific Inquiry

Key Idea 1—The central purpose of scientific inquiry is to develop explanations of natural phenomena in a continuing, creative process. Students need to be able to pose questions independently about natural phenomena. The questions should be clear enough that they can be investigated either in the natural world or by using a model to represent the phenomenon being studied.

Students also need to be able to tell the difference between observations, inferences, predictions, and explanations. Each student needs to be able, after some investigation, to present his or her ideas to others, including fellow students, teachers, and scientists, and determine if their thinking helps others understand his or her findings.

Key Idea 2—Beyond the use of reasoning and consensus, scientific inquiry involves the testing of proposed explanations involving the use of conventional techniques and procedures and usually requiring considerable ingenuity. Students need to be able to use accepted scientific techniques and those of their own design to investigate a problem. Some of these techniques include measuring, observing, describing, and collecting and classifying samples.

Students will need to design a controlled experiment, identify variables, and choose the appropriate number of trials and sample size to ensure a fair test. Students will need to practice safety procedures while conducting their own experiment or an experiment designed by others.

Key Idea 3—The observations made while testing proposed explanations, when analyzed using conventional and invented methods, provide new insights into phenomena. Students need to be able to design charts, tables, graphs, and other ways to present the information collected during an investigation. Students will need to accurately collect and interpret data, using it to evaluate their original hypothesis.

Students will need to be able to form and defend logical arguments about cause and effect relationships in their investigations. If necessary, they will need to suggest improvements and recommendations for further study.

Engineering Design

Key Idea 1 – Engineering design is an iterative process involving modeling and optimization (finding the best solution within given constraints); this process is used to develop technological solutions to problems within given constraints. Students need to be able to identify needs and opportunities for technological solutions from an investigation. In order to do this, they will need to use all available information systems to research the solutions. Working individually and in groups, students will need to design several alternative solutions.

Looking at several possibilities, students will need to evaluate the alternatives, design and construct a model of the product or process, and test the solutions against the specifications outlined.

Standard 4—The Living Environment. This standard includes seven Key Ideas:

Key Idea 1 – Living things are both similar to and different from each other and nonliving things. Students need to know the different parts of plants, animals, and one-celled organisms and the functions of the major human organ systems.

Key Idea 2 – Organisms inherit genetic information in a variety of ways that result in continuity of structure and function between parents and offspring. Students need to know the sexual and asexual mechanisms for passing genetic information from one generation to the next and the ways physical traits are inherited.

Key Idea 3 – Individual organisms and species change over time. Students need to know about variations in organisms and how they help the organism survive. They also need to know about the reasons and importance of competition within species.

Key Idea 4 – The continuity of life is sustained through reproduction and development. Students need to know how different organisms reproduce, including asexual and sexual reproduction. Students also need to know the developmental patterns of several different kinds of plants and animals. Finally, they need to be able to describe cell division at the microscopic level.

Key Idea 5 – Organisms maintain a dynamic equilibrium that sustains life. Students need to know about the ways different organisms carry out basic life functions and maintain equilibrium. They also need to explain the importance of nutrients, vitamins, and minerals in maintaining good health.

Key Idea 6 – Plants and animals depend on each other and their physical environment. Students need to know how matter and energy flow through food chains and food webs and the role of green plants in providing this energy.

Key Idea 7 – Human decisions and activities have had a profound impact on the physical and living environment. Students need to know that living things, including humans, depend on the living and nonliving environment for their survival, and that environmental changes effect humans and other populations.

Standard 4—The Physical Setting. This standard includes five Key Ideas:

Key Idea 1 – The Earth and celestial phenomena can be described by principles of relative motion and perspective. Students need to explain daily, monthly, and seasonal changes on Earth. They also need to know about the motions of the objects in the solar system like the Sun, the Moon, and the planets and stars and how they relate to the Earth.

Key Idea 2 – Many of the phenomena that we observe on Earth involve interactions among components of air, water, and land. Students need to know how the atmosphere (air), hydrosphere (water), and lithosphere (land) interact, evolve, and change. They need to know about erosion and the movement of tectonic plates. They also need to describe volcano and earthquake patterns, the rock and water cycles, and weather and climate changes.

Key Idea 3 – Matter is made up of particles whose properties determine the observable characteristics of matter and its reactivity. Students need to know about the properties of materials, such as density, conductivity, and solubility. They also need to know the difference between chemical and physical changes and be able to explain some common chemical reactions and changes in states of matter.

Key Idea 4 – Energy exists in many forms, and when these forms change energy is conserved. Students need to know the sources of energy transformations in everyday life. They also need to observe and describe heating and cooling events and energy changes as they relate to chemical reactions. Finally, students need to describe the properties of sound, light, magnetism, and electricity and show that they understand the principle of conservation of energy.

Key Idea 5 – Energy and matter interact through forces that result in changes in motion. Students need to describe different patterns of motion of objects and describe and compare the effects of forces (gravity, electric current, and magnetism) on that motion.

Conceptual and Hands-On Skills. In addition to the skills listed above, students will also need to possess a varied set of conceptual and "hands-on skills":

The general skills that students need include:

- Following safety procedures in the classroom and laboratory
- Safely and accurately using the following measurement tools:
  metric ruler
  balance
  stop watch
  graduated cylinder
  thermometer

spring scale

voltmeter

- Using appropriate units for measured or calculated values
- Recognizing and analyzing patterns and trends
- Classifying objects according to an established scheme and a student-generated scheme
- Developing and using a dichotomous key
- Sequencing events
- Identifying cause-and-effect relationships
- Using indicators and interpreting results

In addition, there are several skills that are specific to the Living Environment standard.

They include:

- Manipulating a compound microscope to view microscopic objects
- Determining the size of a microscopic object using a compound microscope
- Preparing a wet mount slide
- Using appropriate staining techniques
- Designing and using a Punnett square or a pedigree chart to predict the probability of certain traits
- Classifying living things according to a student-generated scheme and an established scheme
- Interpreting and/or illustrating the energy flow in a food chain, energy pyramid, or food web
- Identifying pulse points and pulse rates
- Identifying structure and function relationships in organisms

Finally, students should be able to perform the following skills that are specific to the Physical Setting standard:

- Indicating a location's position on a map given the latitude and longitude of the location
- Using identification tests and a flow chart to identify mineral samples
- Using a diagram of the rock cycle to determine geological processes that led to the formation of a specific rock type
- Plotting the location of recent earthquake and volcanic activity on a map and identify patterns of distribution
- Using a magnetic compass to find cardinal directions
- Measuring the angular elevation of an object using appropriate instruments
- Generating and interpreting field maps including topographic and weather maps

- Predicting the characteristics of an air mass based on the origin of the air mass
- Measuring weather variables such as wind speed and direction, relative humidity, barometric pressure, etc.
- Determining the density of liquids, and regular and irregular shaped solids
- Determining the volume of a regular and irregular shaped solid using water displacement
- Using the Periodic Table to identify an element as a metal, nonmetal, or noble gas
- Determining the identity of an unknown element using physical and chemical properties
- Using appropriate resources to separate the parts of a mixture
- Determining the electrical conductivity of a material using a simple circuit
- Determining the speed and acceleration of a moving object

STANDARD 1
Analysis, Inquiry, and Design

Science is more than a mass of facts. It is a way of getting knowledge of the natural world.

Scientists need to know how to collect and interpret information before they can really understand the world around them. Everyone is a scientist at one time or another. So we all need to be able to pose questions, gather and analyze data, come to some conclusions, and begin the process again if necessary.

Standard 1 of the *New York Learning Standards for Mathematics, Science, and Technology* lists what you should know in this important area of science. (If you want to know more about the New York Standards, look at the section called "To the Teacher.") So in this part of the book, you will review and answer questions about the methods of science. These are the things you should know and be able to do in order to investigate important issues in the world around you. Keep in mind that mathematical analysis, scientific inquiry, and technological design involve "higher-order thinking skills." These skills will require you to analyze and evaluate information and put facts together in new ways that make sense for you.

EXAMPLE 1 Reading a Bar Graph

A group of students wanted to study the effect of fertilizer on plant growth. Their results are shown in the graph below:

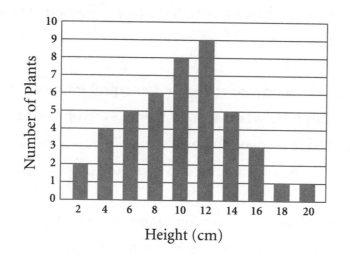

What is the total number of plants with a height of 10 cm?

_____

 **Discussion**

• •

This question is not really a test of how much you know about plants. It tests whether you know how to read a bar graph.

To find the answer, start by reading along the x-axis (the horizontal, left-to-right line at the base of the graph). Continue until you find the bar for plants with a height of 10 cm.

Go to the top of that bar, and read straight across to the y-axis (the vertical, up-and-down line at the left of the graph). You should be able to see that there are 8 plants with a height of 10 cm.

Give yourself a little extra practice. How many plants have a height of 6 cm? 14 cm? 20 cm?

EXAMPLE 2 Using Information from a Bar Graph

Here again is the graph you saw in the last question:

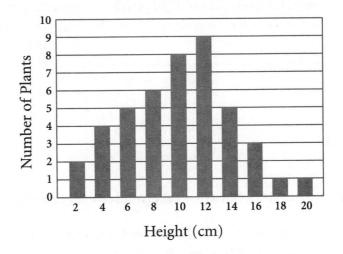

What is the total number of plants studied?

_____

☑ Discussion

Once again, this is a graph-reading question. You need to find the number of plants for each height given. Then you add the values.

Height in cm	Number of plants
2	2
4	4
6	5
8	6
10	8
12	9
14	5
16	3
18	1
20	1

Do the math. There were 44 plants studied.

EXAMPLE 3 **Experimental Design**

The students set one group of plants aside and did not fertilize them. In all other ways, however, this group of plants was treated like the fertilized plants. What is the name for the group of plants that were set aside?

_____

 **Discussion**

• •

In most experiments, scientists start out with several identical setups.

- In one group of setups, called the **experimental group**, something is changed or varied in different ways, and the results are noted.

- The remaining setups, called the **control group**, are left alone.

In this experiment, the plants in the experimental group are fertilized. The fertilizer is the **variable**. In this example, the students would compare any change in plant growth in the experimental group with the growth in the control group. If everything else in the two groups is kept the same, the students could be reasonably sure that it was the fertilizer that was making the difference.

EXAMPLE 4 Interpreting a Data Table

Some students were interested in comparing the heating rate of soil with the heating rate of water. Their experimental set-up included two heat lamps, two one-gallon pails, two thermometers, a sample of soil, a sample of water, and a timer.

The students heated the water and the soil with the heat lamps and took temperature readings of each every minute for 8 minutes. Their data table is shown below:

Time (min)	0	1	2	3	4	5	6	7	8
Soil temp. (°C)	20	21	22.5	24	26	27.5	29.5	30.5	32
Water temp. (°C)	20	21.5	23	23.5	24	25.5	26	27.5	28.5

A. You are at a beach with white sand. At 9 a.m. you measure the temperature of the water and of the sand. They are both 17° C. The weather conditions are clear and sunny all day. Based on the data above, state your prediction about the temperature of the sand compared with that of the water at 2 p.m.

_____

_____

_____

B. Why?

_____

_____

_____

C. What conditions might exist that would make the prediction wrong?

_____

_____

_____

_____

✓ Discussion

A. The sand would be hotter than the water.

B. The data table shows that in the first experiment, the soil heated up more quickly and stayed hotter (32 degrees compared to 28.5 degrees) over the 8 minutes. You might predict that the same phenomenon would happen with sand and water at the beach.

C. There are a number of variables that cannot be controlled at the beach, including size of samples, wind, salt water, white sand (instead of dark soil), particle size (sand is not the same as soil), and movement of the ocean waves and currents. Some or all of these conditions might contribute to different results.

The answer to question C brings up an important point. Nature doesn't always follow the predictions of lab experiments. Nature is messy. In nature, there are a number of interactions going on at all times. It's true that when scientists perform experiments in the laboratory—or in situations they have designed to model what is happening in nature—they can often make very good predictions based on their data. They understand, however, that more tests need to be done in the actual setting before definite conclusions can be drawn. This is why, for example, drugs must be tested on volunteers—people—to determine if they do the job they are supposed to do and are fully safe for patients to use. Not all decisions can be made in the laboratory without additional information from the outside world.

Scientists also know that information they have gathered and decisions they have made can always be changed. Time goes on, and more information is gathered by their colleagues during their research. Some scientific "facts" that people were certain about a hundred years ago have been modified or proved wrong, partly because we have made so many advances in instrumentation (like microscopes and computers). In years to come, many of the ideas we believe to be true will almost certainly be revised and refined by other scientists.

EXAMPLE 5 | Choosing Appropriate Lab Instruments

Here are four instruments used in a laboratory:

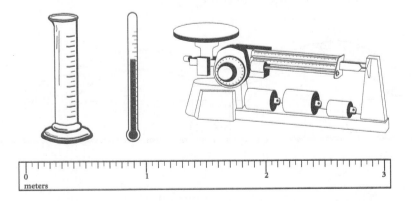

Which instrument would be used to measure the mass of a bird?

1   graduated cylinder

2   metric rule

3   thermometer

4   balance

☑ Discussion

1. A **graduated cylinder** measures the volume of a liquid.

2. A **metric ruler** measures length.

3. A **thermometer** measures temperature. Thermometers can measure degrees on either the Celsius, Fahrenheit, or Kelvin scales.

4. A **balance** measures mass (the amount of matter in an object).

EXAMPLE 6 | Measuring Accurately

A student wrote in her lab report that the length of the earthworm in the diagram below was 10.4 centimeters.

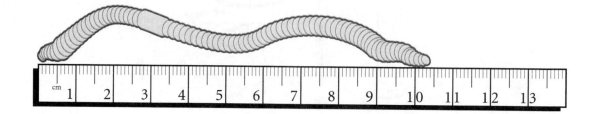

In one or more sentences, explain if this measurement was accurate, and why.

_____

_____

_____

_____

_____

_____

 Discussion

· ·

This measurement was not accurate, because the earthworm is not lying flat against the ruler. It would measure longer if it were lined up properly. However, it should not be stretched out along the ruler, but laid out straight as it would lie naturally.

EXAMPLE 7 | Preparing a Specimen

The diagram below shows a technique used in preparing a specimen for observation with a compound microscope.

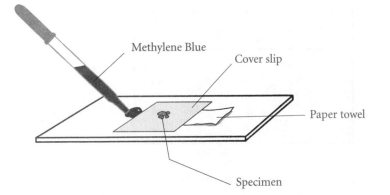

Which technique is shown in the diagram?

1   testing the specimen for starch

2   wetting the specimen

3   sterilizing the specimen

4   staining the specimen

☑ Discussion

The key to the question is noticing that the dropper contains methylene blue.

1. To test a specimen for starch you use iodine or Lugol's solution, not methylene blue.

2. To wet a specimen you use distilled water, not methylene blue.

3   Sterilizing a specimen is not done on a slide. They are sterilized using other techniques, including heat or chemicals like alcohol.

4   Methylene blue is a dye used in staining specimens for examination under the microscope. In staining, a drop of methylene blue (or another stain) is placed at one edge of the cover slip. A small piece of absorbent paper towel is placed at the opposite side of the cover slip to draw the stain across the slide and through the specimen. Once the specimen is stained, the scientist can more easily see the structures within the specimen.

EXAMPLE 8 | Graphs and Data Tables

A student measured the depth of snowfall every hour during a recent storm. The data is shown on the table below:

Time	Depth of Snow
2:00 p.m.	4.0 cm
3:00 p.m.	6.0 cm
4:00 p.m.	8.0 cm
5:00 p.m.	10.0 cm

Which graph best represents the data?

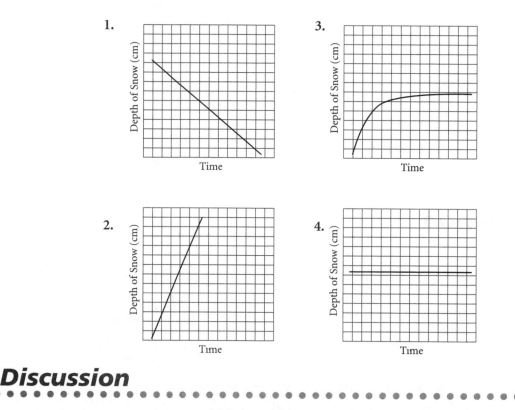

✓ *Discussion*

The data show that the depth of snow kept increasing over time from 4 cm to 10 cm at a rate of 2 cm an hour. Only one graph shows this: the ascending straight-line graph of Choice 2. The other choices do not reflect the data. Graph 1 shows the depth of snow decreasing as time passes. Graph 3 shows the depth of snow increasing, but then leveling off. Graph 4 shows the depth of snow remaining the same over time.

EXAMPLE 9 — Using a Dichotomous Key

While on vacation in Florida, two students collected the specimens pictured below. They all look like ants, but only one of them is a real ant. Use the key below, and label each picture.

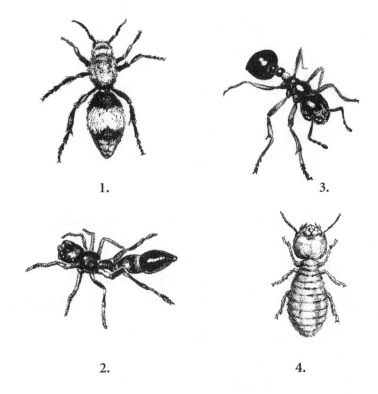

1.

3.

2.

4.

Use the following key to identify the specimens, shown above, that the students collected.

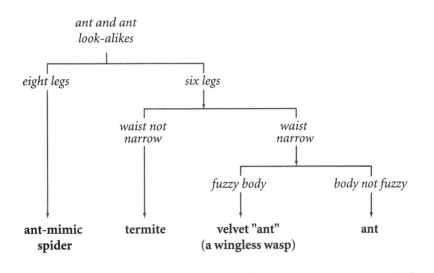

 **Discussion**

This is an example of a *dichotomous* key (pronounced **die KOT-a-mus**; rhymes with hippopotamus). Here's how it works:

Pick a specimen. Start at the top of the key, and look at the two choices just below it. The choice that describes the specimen is the one you want. Then look at the choices below it and pick one—and so on. Keep following the branches until you reach the end.

Specimen 1 –   Does it have six legs or eight?
                        six

                   Is its waist narrow or not narrow?
                        narrow

                   Is its body fuzzy or not-fuzzy ?
                        fuzzy

                   Therefore it is a velvet ant—a wingless wasp, and not a true ant.

Specimen 2 –   Does it have six legs or eight?
                        eight

                   Therefore it is a spider that mimics ants, not a true ant at all

Specimen 3 –   Does it have six legs or eight?
                        six

                   Is its waist narrow or not narrow?
                        narrow

                   Is its body fuzzy or not fuzzy ?
                        not fuzzy

                   Therefore it is a true ant.

Specimen 4 –   Does it have six legs or eight?
                        six

                   Is its waist narrow or not narrow?
                        not narrow

                   Therefore it is a termite and not a true ant.

You might like to know some more about these strange creatures that look like ants but are not.

- A **velvet ant**, as we have said, is a wingless female wasp. It is nearly an inch long, is colored bright red and black, is as fuzzy as a bumblebee, and has a truly vicious sting—so bad that it is locally nicknamed "cow killer." The male has wings and doesn't sting at all.

- The **ant mimic** is one of a number of different spiders around the world that look and even act like ants. Some even hold their front legs next to their heads and wave them like feelers. Some of these spiders eat ants, but others don't. Scientists differ on why some of them have evolved to look like ants.

- **Termites** are sometimes called "white ants," and like ants they live in colonies consisting of a queen, soldiers, and workers. However, they are much more closely related to cockroaches than to true ants. They are terrific eaters of wood, thanks to bacteria and protists in their guts that can digest cellulose for them. If they are not stopped, termites attacking a wooden house can reduce it to dust in a couple of years.

Once again—this is not a question that tests how much you know about insects. It is a test to see if you can read a key of this kind when it describes an unfamiliar subject.

However, if you remember **never** to touch a fuzzy, red-and-black "ant," that will be a real plus!

STANDARD 4
Science
Part I: *The Living Environment*

The *Living Environment* part of Standard 4 deals with the life sciences. It includes 7 Key Ideas, or important areas you should be familiar with, in biology and the environmental sciences. (If you want to know more about these Key Ideas, look at "The Living Environment" under the List of Standards in the section called "To the Teacher." It's near the beginning of this book.)

The questions that follow will help you review what you should know in this important area of science.

EXAMPLE 1 Levels of Complexity

The diagram below shows the organization of a multicellular organism:

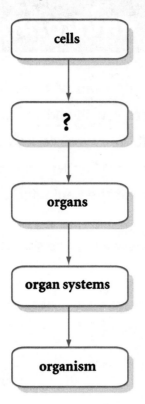

Which label is needed to fill in the second box and complete the diagram?

1   atoms

2   organelles

3   nerves

4   tissues

☑ *Discussion*

The diagram shows the organization of an organism according to levels of complexity, from cells to the complete organism. Below are discussions of each answer choice.

1 **Atoms** are the basic building blocks of all ordinary matter, including the molecules that make up cells. They would not be placed in the diagram between *cells* and *organs*. They would have to be placed in an expanded diagram at a level considerably before *cells*.

2 **Organelles** are <u>parts</u> of cells. They perform specialized functions similar to those performed by the organs of a multicellular organism. However, since they are parts of cells, they would appear in an expanded diagram at the level just before *cells*.

3 **Nerves** are special organs that carry messages between the central nervous system and different parts of the body. They are not a "level of organization" like cells or organs or organ systems.

4 **Tissues** are groups of cells that are similar and that are organized to perform some function. They should be placed in the box between cells and organs.

EXAMPLE 2 | Similarities in Plants and Animals

Which statement below is true for both plants and animals?

1   They use muscles for movement.

2   They make their own food.

3   They are made up of cells.

4   They are producers.

 **Discussion**

• •

Some of these statements are true of plants and some are true of animals. Only one is true for both.

1   Only animals have **muscles**.

2   Only green plants, those with chlorophyll, can make their own food. They do this using the process known as **photosynthesis**.

3   All living things, both plants and animals, are **made up of cells**.

4   Only plants can make their own food. So they are **producers**. Animals must eat to obtain food. They are consumers.

EXAMPLE 3 Systems of the Body

What is the system shown in the diagram below, and what is its function?

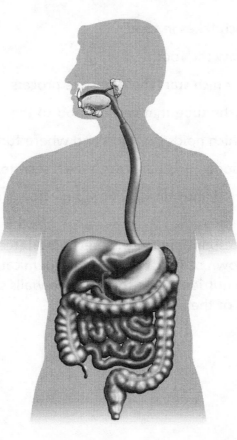

_____

_____

_____

_____

_____

_____

_____

_____

☑ Discussion

This is a diagram of the **digestive system**. The diagram shows all of the following:

- the mouth, which takes in food

- teeth, which chew the food

- salivary glands, which start the digestive process

- the esophagus, the tube that carries food to the stomach

- the stomach, which holds the food and where further digestion takes place

- the liver, gallbladder, and pancreas, which secrete special digestive juices

- the large and small intestines, where digestion is concluded and solid wastes are formed.

The digestive system is responsible for the mechanical (teeth) and chemical (saliva and digestive juices) breakdown of food into simpler chemical components. In their simpler, broken-down form, the nutrients pass through the walls of the intestines and are transported to all living cells of the body.

EXAMPLE 4 | Organs in an Organ System

Which group of structures is part of the system that transports nutrients and gases throughout the body?

1   muscles, bones, cartilage

2   heart, capillaries, veins

3   tongue, esophagus, stomach

4   brain, endocrine glands, nerves

Discussion

Each of the answer choices above lists organs that belong to a particular organ system.

1   **Muscles, bones, and cartilage** are parts of the skeletal and muscular systems. These systems are coordinated by the nervous system and are necessary for loco-motion. Animals must be able to move to escape danger, obtain food and shelter, and reproduce the species.

2   The **heart, capillaries, and veins** are parts of the circulatory system. The heart pumps blood around the body The blood carries oxygen from the lungs and nutri-ents from the intestines to the organs for growth, cell repair, and cellular respira-tion. Capillaries are the smallest blood vessels, carrying blood cells to all tissues where gas exchange (carbon dioxide and oxygen) take place. Veins carry blood back to the heart. From there the blood is pumped to the lungs, where oxygen is replenished and carbon dioxide is released and exhaled.

3   As discussed in the previous example, the **tongue, esophagus, and stomach** are all organs in the digestive system. The tongue pushes food back into the esophagus. This is the tube through which the partially broken-down and digested food pass-es to the stomach. In the stomach the food, especially proteins, continues to be broken down and digested.

4   The **brain, spinal cord, and nerves** act together to direct messages to various parts of the body. The endocrine glands release chemicals called hormones into the blood stream. Hormones bring about reactions in various organs. Together, these two systems, nervous and endocrine, maintain a balance among the activities of all the different organ systems.

EXAMPLE 5 | **Circulation of Blood**

The diagram below shows the circulation of blood around the human body. Fill in the blanks to indicate the name of the organ whose function is described.

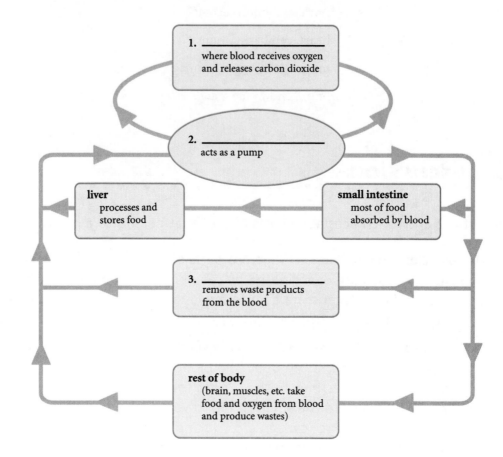

1. _____
where blood receives oxygen
and releases carbon dioxide

2. _____
acts as a pump

liver
processes and
stores food

small intestine
most of food
absorbed by blood

3. _____
removes waste products
from the blood

rest of body
(brain, muscles, etc. take
food and oxygen from blood
and produce wastes)

 **Discussion**

1. The **lungs** are the paired organs where the blood receives oxygen and releases carbon dioxide.

2. The **heart** acts as a pump to move blood through the body.

3. The **kidneys** remove water and waste products from the blood.

EXAMPLE 6 Constructing a Punnett Square

Pea plants have a recessive gene for wrinkled seeds and a dominant gene for plump seeds. If a pure wrinkled seed plant were crossed with a pure plump seed plant, which of the following statements would be true of the offspring?

1   all would produce plump seeds

2   all would produce wrinkled seeds

3   more would produce plump seeds than wrinkled seeds

4   more would produce wrinkled seeds than plump seeds

Construct a Punnett square to help you with your answer.

☑ *Discussion*

All the offspring would produce plump seeds, because each offspring pea plant contains a dominant gene for plump seeds. Since wrinkling is a recessive trait, it will not show up in the offspring in this generation. There would be no wrinkled seeds at all, not just fewer than the number of plump seeds.

The result of the cross can be shown in the following diagram, called a Punnett square:

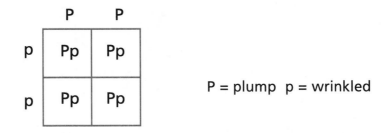

P = plump p = wrinkled

- The plump-seed parent has two copies of the gene for plumpness (P), as shown above the square.

- The wrinkle-seed parent has two copies of the gene for wrinkling (p), as shown in the column to the left of the square.

- Each of the four compartments of the square is filled in with the result of the combination of the gene above it and the gene to the left of it.

The Punnett square shows that all combinations are Pp. Since the P allele is dominant, all the seeds of the offspring will be plump.

EXAMPLE 7 Causes of Extinction

The animal shown below is the largest land mammal that ever existed. It was a kind of giant hornless rhinoceros, and it was much bigger than the largest elephant. It no longer exists, for it became extinct over 20 million years ago.

For which of the following reasons might an organism become extinct?

1   It cannot adjust to a changing environment.

2   It relies too much on the sun's energy to make food.

3   It gives birth to too many offspring.

4   It eats only food made by other organisms.

✓ Discussion

1   Organisms that do not have adaptive characteristics that allow them to adjust to changes in the environment will become extinct.

2   Organisms that rely on the sun's energy to make food for themselves are plants, essential parts of an ecosystem. Using photosynthesis to make food does not affect whether or not an organism might become extinct.

3   Organisms usually do produce too many offspring. But this does not lead to extinction. Only the strongest and most fit survive and reproduce the next generation. This characteristic is a protection against extinction.

4   Organisms that eat food made by other organisms are primary consumers, also called herbivores or plant eaters. They are an important link in the food chain. A herbivore might possibly become extinct if its food supply was no longer available in the environment, and it did not adapt to use some other food source. But this is not just because it was a plant-eater.

Use the diagram below to answer Examples 8–10. It shows the series of changes a frog goes through during reproduction and development.

EXAMPLE 8 **Methods of Reproduction**

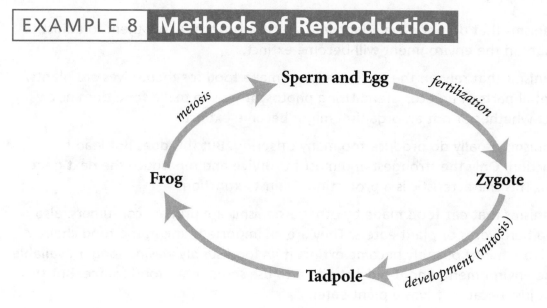

What type of reproduction is represented in this diagram?

1   sexual

2   asexual

3   migratory

4   dominant

✔️ Discussion

• •

1   In **sexual reproduction**, as shown in the diagram, there are two parents. One parent contributes sperm, and the other contributes an egg. Each parent contributes half of the genetic material of the offspring.

2   In **asexual reproduction**, such as happens in ordinary cell division (mitosis) or in spore formation, there is only one parent. All the offspring's genes come from this single parent. The offspring is thus genetically identical to the parent.

3   **Migratory** is not a form of reproduction. It is a description of animals that periodically (usually seasonally) move to locations with more favorable conditions.

4   **Dominant** is not a form of reproduction, either. It describes a form (allele) of a gene whose characteristic is always expressed.

EXAMPLE 9 | Mitosis and Meiosis

Compare the amount of genetic material in an adult frog's cells with the amount in the sperm or egg cell. Explain.

_____

_____

_____

_____

_____

_____

_____

 Discussion

The amount of genetic material in the sperm or egg cell is one-half that of the parent's cells. The sex cells have undergone a special kind of cell division called **meiosis**, in which the parent cell's genetic material is divided between the two daughter cells. This is very different from ordinary cell division, or **mitosis**, in which each of the daughter cells gets the full amount of the parent cell's genetic material.

EXAMPLE 10 | From Tadpole to Frog

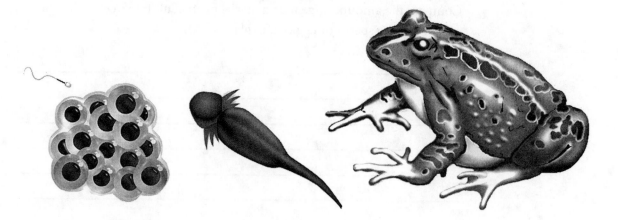

The process in which a tadpole grows into a frog is called

1   asexual reproduction

2   external fertilization

3   metamorphosis

4   respiration

 **Discussion**

● ●

1   **Asexual reproduction** is a process in which offspring are produced from only one parent. It has nothing to do with the transformation of a tadpole into a frog.

2   **External fertilization** has nothing to do with the tadpole–frog transformation, either. It is a process in which eggs are fertilized by sperm outside the mother's body. Many fish—salmon, for example—reproduce this way. The female deposits her eggs in a stream, and the male squirts his sperm over them.

3   **Metamorphosis** is the process in which organisms change form as they develop into adults. The transformation of a tadpole into a frog is one example. So is the transformation of a caterpillar into a butterfly.

4   **Respiration** is the process in which the body takes in and uses oxygen. In ordinary usage, *respiration* means breathing. Scientists also speak of *cellular respiration*, the process in which cells use oxygen to release energy stored in food. It has nothing to do with the change of a tadpole into a frog.

Use the information in the chart below to answer Examples 11–12.

EXAMPLE 11   Reading a Food Chart

A patient was advised by his doctor to reduce the amount of fat in his diet. He was given the chart below and told to choose those foods which are high in protein and carbohydrates and low in fats.

1. According to the data, which is based on a 100g sample of each food, which foods are good sources of —

   a) proteins?

   b) carbohydrates?

Type of Food	Proteins	Fats	Carbohydrates
white bread	8.1	1.7	54.3
wheat bread	9.6	3.1	46.7
butter	0.5	81.0	0.0
cheese	25.4	34.5	0.0
milk	3.3	3.8	4.8
roast chicken	24.8	5.4	0.0
pork chops	28.5	24.2	0.0
cabbage	1.7	0.0	2.3
carrots	0.7	0.0	5.4
banana	1.1	0.0	19.4

Foods high in protein:

_____

Foods high in carbohydrates:

_____

 **Discussion**

For **proteins**, cheese (25.4 g), roast chicken (24.8 g), and pork chops (28.5 g) have much more protein than the other foods listed.

For **carbohydrates**, white bread (54.3 g), wheat bread (46.7 g), and bananas (19.2 g) have more carbohydrates than the other foods listed.

EXAMPLE 12	**Comparing Values in a Food Chart**

One possible diet includes roast chicken. According to the chart in Example 11, is roast chicken better than a pork chop when a person is trying to reduce fat intake? Explain your answer.

_____

_____

_____

_____

_____

_____

_____

_____

 *Discussion*

Pork chops contain almost 5 times as much fat as roast chicken does. According to the chart, roast chicken contains 5.4 grams of fat in every 100 gram sample and pork chops contain 24.2 grams of fat. So, according to the information in the chart, roast chicken is a better choice than pork chops.

EXAMPLE 13 Transmission of Disease

Some diseases are caused by microscopic organisms and may be transmitted from one individual to another. These diseases are called

1 genetic

2 infectious

3 allergic

4 hormonal

 Discussion

1. **Genetic diseases** are transferred from parent to offspring. However, they are not caused by microorganisms—they are caused by defects in the genetic material in the sperm or egg cells.

2. **Infectious diseases** are caused by microscopic bacteria or viruses. They can be acquired from contaminated water, dirt, insect bites, and other means. Some infectious diseases can be spread from one person to another. These are called contagious diseases. There are vaccines to protect against some infectious diseases, such as measles and polio.

3. Although many people and animals suffer from **allergies**, they cannot be spread from one individual to another. Allergies are an over-reaction of the body to a stimulus such as pollen, insect stings, or certain foods. The symptoms of the reaction are usually sneezing, runny nose, and swollen eyes.

4. **Hormonal diseases** are not spread from one individual to another except sometimes through heredity. They are usually caused by a malfunction of a feedback mechanism within the body. An example of a hormonal disease is diabetes. In diabetes, not enough insulin is produced by the pancreas. Insulin regulates the metabolism of blood sugar, glucose, so in diabetes increased levels of glucose appear in the blood.

EXAMPLE 14   Photosynthesis

Green plants undergo an essential process called **photosynthesis.**

a. Explain the process of photosynthesis. Be sure to identify all of the components of the process as well as all the products.

_____

_____

_____

_____

_____

_____

b. Explain why photosynthesis is important to an individual plant and to an entire ecosystem.

_____

_____

_____

_____

_____

_____

☑ Discussion

· ·

a. **Photosynthesis** is the process by which plants (and certain chlorophyll-containing bacteria) use the energy of sunlight to make their own food, a sugar called *glucose*, from water and carbon dioxide in the atmosphere. The process is made possible by the green pigment chlorophyll in the cells of the plant. In the process, oxygen is released. The entire process can be represented by the equation:

$$\text{carbon dioxide} + \text{water} \xrightarrow[\text{chlorophyll}]{\text{light}} \text{glucose} + \text{oxygen}$$

b. **Photosynthesis** is important to the plant itself because it uses the food made in the process food, glucose, for its own growth and development. Photosynthesis is essential for an entire ecosystem because all animals depend on the plants for their energy needs as well. Without plants, no animals would survive.

EXAMPLE 15	Life Processes in Plants

Which process is shown in the following drawing?

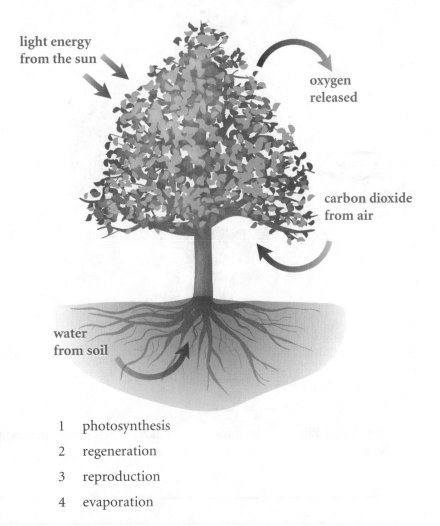

1   photosynthesis

2   regeneration

3   reproduction

4   evaporation

 **Discussion**

1   **Photosynthesis** is the process used by green plants to use light energy, carbon dioxide, and water to make food. It is shown in the drawing above.

2   **Regeneration** is the process that some organisms use to replace lost body parts. It is not shown in the drawing.

3   **Reproduction** is the process by which offspring are produced. It is not shown in the drawing.

4   **Evaporation** occurs when a liquid changes to a gas. It is not shown in the drawing.

EXAMPLE 16 **Food Web**

The diagram below shows a simplified food web.

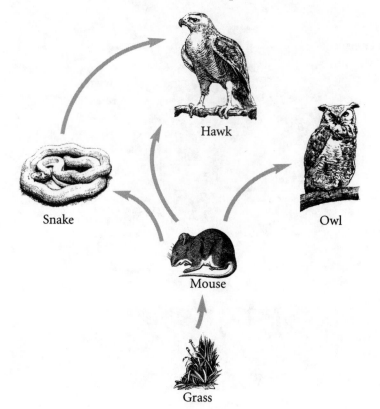

Hawk

Snake

Owl

Mouse

Grass

If a disease killed all the mice, what is likely to happen to the owl population? Why?

_____

_____

_____

_____

_____

_____

 **Discussion**

The owl population would decrease because its food supply, the mice, is no longer available.

EXAMPLE 17 **Decomposers**

The most important role of decomposers in an ecosystem is their ability to

1   return dead plant and animal nutrients to the soil

2   convert the sun's light energy into stored energy

3   withstand extreme temperature and drought conditions

4   serve as a major food source for animals

✓ *Discussion*

1   The function of decomposers, such as bacteria and fungi, is to break down plant and animal matter. The nutrients stored in that matter return to the soil to be available for plants.

2   Converting the sun's light energy into stored energy is the role of green plants, the producers, through the process of photosynthesis. Decomposers cannot photosynthesize.

3   Like all living organisms, decomposers function best within specific temperature ranges. Some of them may be able to withstand extreme temperatures or drought conditions, but that is not their most important role.

4   Decomposers are not a major food source for animals. Animals usually eat only plants (herbivores) or only animals (carnivores). Some, like most humans, eat both plants and animals and are called omnivores. But not many animals subsist on mushrooms, molds, or soil bacteria.

EXAMPLE 18 Changes in an Ecosystem

In an ecosystem, a virus has infected a large population of small plant-eating rodents, causing most of them to die. As a result, in the next few months, you would expect to observe that

1   new small rodents had immediately taken the place of the infected rodents

2   predators on rodents in the region had started to eat only plants

3   plants once eaten by the infected rodents were becoming more plentiful

4   the entire ecosystem had collapsed

✔ Discussion

1   This is unlikely. Changes in ecosystems take place only gradually. Different small rodents might eventually move in to take the place of the infected ones, but not immediately. In addition, the virus might still be present and might infect the new population of rodents.

2   Animals that preyed on the rodents could not suddenly switch to eating plants. They would be physically unable to live exclusively on plants. For example, a fox's teeth are adapted for biting and tearing, not for grinding grass the way a cow's teeth are.

3   Without another animal in place to eat them, the plants would continue to reproduce and become plentiful. This would continue until the plants began to crowd each other out and use up the available resources.

4   The ecosystem would not collapse. It would gradually adjust, as different organisms moved in to fill the available roles. This adjustment is called "dynamic equilibrium."

EXAMPLE 19 **Researching a Community Problem**

The storage of radioactive wastes is a major concern of the opponents of nuclear power as an energy source for America.

A waste storage company has access to an old mine and proposes to use it to store spent plutonium, a radioactive waste.

The population of the small town near the old mine is split. Many residents see the storage facility as a way to increase employment in the town. Others are worried that the radioactive materials will seep into the water supply and contaminate it.

The waste storage company has assured the community that the facility will be safe and will not pollute the water or land.

You are asked to prepare a report for the community that will enable them to discuss the issue intelligently.

List at least three types of information you would research and present to the community to help them make a decision about this issue.

_____

_____

_____

_____

_____

☑ Discussion

Answers will differ but might include information about any and all of the following:

1. type and amount of radioactive waste

2. the nature and severity of the health hazards caused by radioactive waste of this kind

3. the effectiveness of mines of this type in isolating radioactive waste

4. how close the old mine is to the ground water supply

5 the probability that there might be an existing leak in the mine

6. the geological stability of the area—the probability of earth movements breaking the "seal" provided by the mine

7. types and numbers of jobs created for the community

8. short- and long-range effects on the surrounding environment

9. other uses for the mine that might benefit the community in a less risky way

10. the history of similar efforts elsewhere

11. the reliability of the waste storage company

12. what measures could be taken against the waste storage company if their assurances prove unreliable—and the likelihood of these measures succeeding in reversing the damage

Use the information in Example 20 to answer the questions in Examples 20 through 22.

EXAMPLE 20 An Ecological Investigation

An ecologist is studying the feeding habits of small mammals in the Arizona desert. She wants to find out how four different species of rodents—the kangaroo rat, Arizona pocket mouse, Bailey pocket mouse, and desert pocket mouse—can all eat seeds and survive.

The ecologist decides to investigate two different ideas: A) that each kind of rodent eats a different kind of seed, or B) that they eat in different locations around the desert. She discovers that B is correct—the four species of animals eat the same kinds of seeds, but they eat them in different places.

Explain why the ecologist could be fairly certain that the rodents could not be eating the same kinds of seeds in the same places.

_____

_____

_____

_____

_____

_____

_____

_____

☑ Discussion

The ecologist could be fairly certain that the different rodents were not eating the same seeds in the same places. This is because of a well-known principle in ecology. It involves what scientists call an **ecological niche**. (An ecological niche is an organism's place and role in an ecosystem. It includes what it does, where it lives, how it gets its food, and what it eats.)

The principle is simple. It states: *Two species cannot occupy the same ecological niche.* Organisms are constantly competing with each other. If two species were to compete for the same resources in the same way, one species would be more successful than the other. The less successful species would die out.

So different species are forced to occupy different ecological niches. By doing this, they avoid the kind of ruinous competition that would take place if they occupied the same ecological niche. So they do not do the same things in the same way. The four species under investigation could not be eating the same kinds of seeds in the same places.

EXAMPLE 21 | An Ecological Investigation—2

Describe a procedure this scientist could use to determine which types of seeds are eaten by each of the animals in Example 20.

_____

_____

_____

_____

_____

_____

_____

_____

 **Discussion**

• •

The ecologist would have to establish a procedure that would allow her to know how many and which kinds of seeds each animal ate. One way would be to provide each of the animals with several different kinds of seeds from a variety of different desert plants, including big and little seeds, high- and low-protein seeds, and oily and dry seeds. Then she would need to observe which animals ate which kinds of seeds and keep a chart of her observations so she could analyze them later.

There are other possible ways, but this is the one used by the scientist who did the study.

EXAMPLE 22 | Characteristics that Promote Survival

When the ecologist observed kangaroo rats in the desert, she discovered that they were not as good at finding seeds under leaves and sticks as mice were, but when the seeds were in the open spaces, the kangaroo rats could find and eat them faster than the other rodents.

What do ecologists call a characteristic like this—something that enables a living organism to survive and reproduce in its particular environment? What advantage does it give to the individual organism? What is the advantage to the species?

_____

_____

_____

_____

_____

_____

_____

_____

 **Discussion**

Those properties of living things that enable them to survive and reproduce in an environment are called **adaptations**. When an organism is better at some activity than another organism is, it is said to be better adapted for that activity. In this case, the kangaroo rats were better adapted to finding seeds in the open spaces and eating them quickly. This characteristic helps a rat because it can find its food quickly, before predators find it! Also, if there are other kangaroo rats in the area, the best-adapted rat finds its food fastest.

Adaptations help the species survive because the organisms that are better adapted tend to have the most and best-adapted offspring. In the example, the kangaroo rats that find food most quickly will survive and be able to pass their genes on to future generations. The slower members of the species will not get food as quickly, and they may not get as much. Before they can reproduce, they may die of starvation or be killed by predators. In either case, their less well-adapted genes will not be passed on to offspring.

Base your answers to questions 23 through 25 on the reading passage below and on your knowledge of the living environment.

EXAMPLE 23 | Modes of Obtaining Food

About 70 years ago the Welland Canal was built between Lake Ontario and Lake Erie. Ships could move from the St. Lawrence River, around Niagara Falls, to the rest of the Great Lakes. But the canal also allowed plants and animals to swim or be transported on the hulls of ships into the Great Lakes. The sea lamprey was one of those animals.

The lamprey looks something like an eel. It has slimy brownish skin, a long body, tail, and two single fins on top. It can grow to be 60 centimeters long and weigh about 500 grams. The lamprey's head has a small undeveloped eye on each side and a nasal opening to help it smell. There are seven open gill slits on each side of the head that open to pouches with feathery gills inside.

Instead of a jaw, the lamprey has a circular mouth like a funnel that is lined with many sharp teeth. Its tongue has sharp projections as well. This mouth is well adapted for the lamprey to attach to a host fish, tear a hole into the fish's body, and suck out the blood and other body fluids. When the fish dies, the lamprey moves on to another host fish.

Lampreys feed mostly on lake trout, but they attack many other kinds of fish as well. The fish population in the Great Lakes has been greatly reduced since the lamprey arrived.

The sea lamprey can best be described as

1 a parasite

2 a producer

3 an herbivore

4 an autotroph

☑ *Discussion*

1   A **parasite** is an organism that obtains its nutrients from another organism on which it lives. This description fits the lamprey.

2   A **producer** is an organism that can make its own food, like a green plant

3   A **herbivore** is an animal that eats green plants

4   An **autotroph** is another name for a producer. It makes its own food. Plants are autotrophs. No animal is.

EXAMPLE 24 **Causes of Ecological Change**

The movement of the sea lamprey into the Great Lakes is an example of

1   environmental changes brought about by humans

2   impact of global warming

3   radioactive waste disposal

4   urban growth

☑ *Discussion*

1   The sea lamprey entered the Great Lakes ecosystem through a canal. This environmental change was brought about by humans. Humans made the decision to increase transportation between the Midwest and the Northeast by building a canal. At the time the decision was made, people were less aware than they are now of how quickly organisms can move into a new ecosystem and of how damaging to the ecosystem this can be.

2   The impact of global warming is an important environmental problem. It is probably caused by increased amounts of carbon dioxide in the atmosphere which trap the Sun's heat, raising temperatures around the Earth. But it has nothing to do with the movements of the sea lamprey.

3   Radioactive waste disposal causes concern about the environment. Nuclear energy, some argue, is clean and efficient. However, after a time, the radioactive material used to generate the energy is nearly used up and must be disposed of. Environmentalists feel that this material may still spill some of its poisonous radioactivity into water supplies; that would threaten the health of many people living in the area. But again, this has nothing to do with the movements of the sea lamprey.

4   Urban growth is a result of a growing population. As more and more communities are built around major cities, trees are cut down, farmland is used for housing developments, and watersheds are drained. More people in a community means more cars, more roads, more waste to be disposed of, and a greater threat to delicate ecosystems like wetlands. Indirectly, it can lead to building larger transportation networks, which might include canals like the one that brought the lamprey into the Great Lakes. But this is a very indirect cause, and not the best answer to the question.

EXAMPLE 25 **Adaptation**

The lamprey uses the blood and body fluids of the host fish for nourishment. Explain how the lamprey's digestive system might be adapted for this way of life.

_____
_____
_____
_____
_____
_____
_____

☑ *Discussion*
• •

The lamprey's digestive system would be very simple, because its food is in liquid form. It is already nearly digested as soon as the lamprey sucks it out.

EXAMPLE 26	**Making an Accurate Identification from a Description**

Based on the description in the passage, which drawing below best represents what a student's laboratory drawing of a sea lamprey should look like?

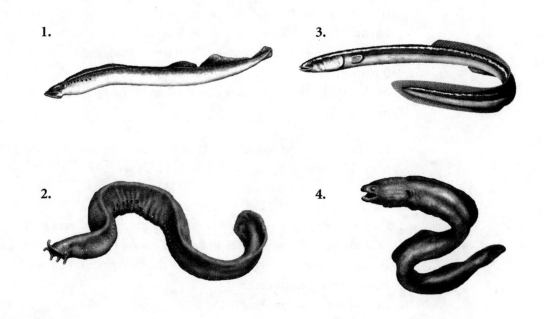

1.

3.

2.

4.

☑ *Discussion*

● ●

Only one drawing shows an organism shaped like an eel, with a circular sucker for a mouth, seven gill openings, two single dorsal fins, and tiny, undeveloped eyes. That drawing, Number 1, is the lamprey. Drawing 2 shows a relative of the lamprey called a hagfish. Drawing 3 shows a real eel. Drawing 4 is a fish called a moray eel. Neither is closely related to a lamprey.

Base your answers to questions 26 and 27 on the reading passage below and on your knowledge of science.

EXAMPLE 27   **Acid Rain**

It's raining sulfuric acid! When you work in the laboratory, you are probably warned to be careful around acids. But these are the very acids that are raining down on parts of Earth, especially in the northeastern United States. Coal-burning plants in the midwest release gases like sulfur dioxide and nitrogen oxides. When these gases are dissolved in rainwater, they form sulfuric acid and nitric acid.

In New York's Adirondack Mountains, many lakes are so acidic they no longer have fish living in them. Acid rain also kills vegetation, resulting in lower crop yields and destroyed forests.

Coal-burning plants are now required to install scrubbers in their smokestacks to clean the poisonous gases out of the smoke before it reaches the atmosphere. However, developing countries across the globe cannot always afford to install this expensive equipment, so acid rain will continue to be a problem.

Think of a food chain and explain how raccoons and otters in the Adirondacks would be affected by acid rain in the lakes.

_____

_____

_____

_____

_____

_____

_____

_____

 **Discussion**

Raccoons and otters—and many other animals and birds as well—eat fish. But many fish—trout, for example—cannot survive in waters made acidic by acid rain. Their food can't survive, either. For example, many fish eat plants. If lakes in an area populated by raccoons and otters become too acidic to support plant life, there will no longer be fish there either. The fish have no food, and they die. If there are no fish in the lakes, the fish-eating animals would have no fish to eat. They would have to change their diet, if possible, or move to another location, or starve.

EXAMPLE 28 | Erosion and Soil Deposition

If forests were killed because of acid rain, what impact would that have on erosion and soil deposition in an area? Explain.

_____

_____

_____

_____

_____

_____

_____

 **Discussion**

Tree roots are important in holding soil in place, especially in mountainous areas where gravity is acting to push soil down the incline of the hill. If the trees die, their roots will no longer hold the soil. It will erode, and the silt will move into rivers and streams, changing their depth and flow. Plants and animals that live in and around the rivers and streams could be affected by this change.

EXAMPLE 29 | Adding Carbon Dioxide to the Atmosphere

Through what biological process do animals add carbon dioxide to the atmosphere? Explain.

_____

_____

_____

_____

_____

_____

_____

 *Discussion*

Animals exhale carbon dioxide into the environment when they breathe. The carbon dioxide is created in the cells of the body. It is a byproduct of body processes that use oxygen. From the cells it is picked up by the blood, which is circulating around the body to deliver nutrients and oxygen to the cells. The blood delivers the carbon dioxide to the lungs. There, the carbon dioxide is exchanged for incoming oxygen and is breathed out into the atmosphere.

Base your answers to questions 30 and 31 on the following reading passage and your knowledge of science.

EXAMPLE 30 | The Greenhouse Effect

What's all the fuss about carbon dioxide in the atmosphere? Carbon dioxide has always been in the atmosphere. In the past hundred years, however, the concentration of carbon dioxide has increased due to the burning of fossil fuels.

When solar energy comes through the atmosphere and strikes the Earth, about a third of it is radiated back into space. About half of the rest is absorbed by the earth and re-emitted as infrared rays—radiant heat. Carbon dioxide is particularly efficient at absorbing this heat.

Now that people are adding so many more carbon dioxide molecules in the atmosphere, those molecules are absorbing more of the infrared rays and radiating them back to Earth again. The result is more energy in the atmosphere, and the Earth heats up. This is called "the greenhouse effect."

Scientists studying the greenhouse effect have predicted that this increased heat will have many effects. It will dry out land and create more deserts. It will melt polar ice caps, and the resulting rise in sea level may cause flooding of coastal cities.

One researcher has investigated how increased carbon dioxide levels will affect plant growth. He has found that the plants grow unusually large and fast. However, the plants themselves have less nutritional value than they do when they grow normally. He fed caterpillars these plants and found that the caterpillars were smaller and died earlier than they do under current conditions.

It is nearly impossible to calculate the long-range effect that global warming may have.

Which biological process uses most of the carbon dioxide in the atmosphere? What is the formula for it?

_____

_____

_____

_____

_____

_____

 **Discussion**
• •

The biological process that uses most of the carbon dioxide in the atmosphere is photosynthesis, the process plants use to make food. The formula is:

$$\text{carbon dioxide + water} \xrightarrow[\text{chlorophyll}]{\text{light}} \text{oxygen + glucose}$$

Remember that chlorophyll and light must be present for this process to take place.

EXAMPLE 31 | Global Warming and Food Webs

Draw a food web using the following organisms and predict what might happen if the caterpillar population were reduced due to global warming.

plants, caterpillars, insect-eating birds, snakes, hawks

_____

_____

_____

_____

_____

_____

☑ *Discussion*

The food web might look something like this:

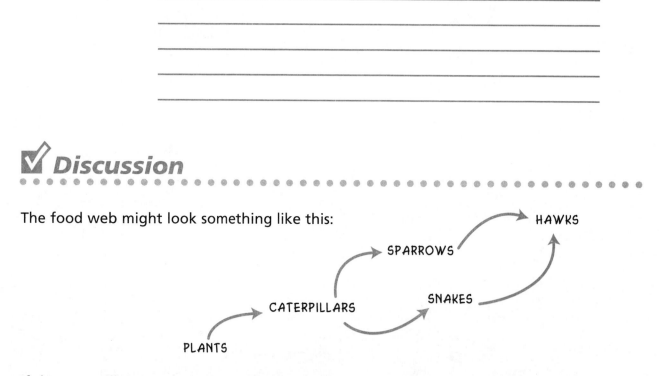

If the caterpillar population were reduced, the snakes and birds would have less to eat. They might die, or they might move to another location. Either way, the hawks' food supply would be limited and they might die.

STANDARD 4
Science
Part 2: *The Physical Setting*

The Physical Setting part of Standard 4 deals with the physical sciences. It is divided into 5 Key Ideas, or important areas you should be familiar with, in earth and space science, chemistry, and physics. (If you want to know more about these Key Ideas, look at "The Physical Setting" under the List of Standards in the section called "To the Teacher." It's near the beginning of this book.)

The questions that follow will help you review what you should know in these important areas of science.

EXAMPLE 1 | **Tides**

At which location in the following diagram would tides be highest?

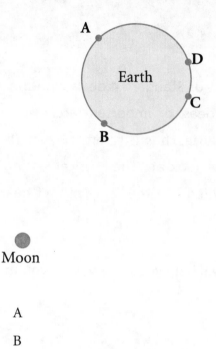

Moon

1 A

2 B

3 C

4 D

✓ Discussion

The gravitational force of the moon pulls outward on Earth's surface, causing the tides. The side closest to the moon is pulled the most, so the tides would be highest at Point B. (They would also be highest at a point on the opposite side of Earth from B.)

The sun also exerts a gravitational pull on Earth, but the moon is closer and has a stronger pull. When the moon and sun are in line, the tides are highest. When the moon and the sun are not in line, the tides are lower. But the tides are always high on the side close to the moon.

EXAMPLE 2 | **The Rotation of the Earth**

The rotation of Earth on its axis is the cause of

1   the seasons

2   the 24-hour day

3   the 365-day year

4   longitude and latitude

✔ Discussion

1   The **seasons** are caused by the tilt of the Earth on its axis, not by its daily rotation. The tilt does not change as Earth moves in its path around the Sun. So the axis always points towards Polaris, the North Star.

2   It takes 24 hours for the Earth to **rotate**, or turn, on its axis—one full day.

3   It takes about 365 days, one year, for Earth to make one **revolution** in its orbit around the sun. This is different from the **rotation** of Earth on its axis. (Notice that we use the word *revolution* to talk about the movement of Earth around the sun, and *rotation* to talk about the spin of Earth around its axis.)

4   Longitude and latitude are lines that form an imaginary grid used to measure distance on Earth.

•   **Longitude** is measured in degrees east and west of a north-south line, the prime meridian (which passes through Greenwich, England).

•   **Latitude** is measured in degrees north and south of the equator.

Neither is "caused" by Earth's rotation.

EXAMPLE 3 | **Classification of Rocks**

Rocks can be classified on the basis of

1 the mass of the sample

2 their age in millions of years

3 the shape of the sample

4 how they were formed

☑ *Discussion*

1 The mass of the sample varies with the size of the sample, so it cannot be used to classify a rock.

2 Rocks of very different ages can be of the same type. For example, one volcanic rock might have been formed hundreds of millions of years ago, while another might have been formed from lava pouring out of a volcano that erupted yesterday. Yet, except for their ages, the two rocks might be almost identical.

3 Rocks are not classified by shape. The shapes of rocks can vary depending on the weathering and erosion they have undergone.

4 Rocks can be formed in one of three ways: by the compressing and cementing of sediments (sedimentary rocks), by heating and forming crystals (metamorphic rocks), or by melting deep within the Earth to form magma and cooling to form crystals (igneous rocks). Almost all rocks fit into one of these three classifications.

The classification of rocks as igneous, sedimentary, or metamorphic is a very broad one. Geologists also use more detailed classifications based on the chemical composition and crystal structure of the minerals that compose the rock.

Base your answers to the questions in Examples 4 and 5 on information from the map and the chart below.

EXAMPLE 4 **Weather Systems**

City	Air Temperature	Weather Conditions
Albany	85°F	overcast
Syracuse	68°F	rain
Buffalo	60°F	clear

What type of pressure system was probably over Buffalo?

1   high

2   low

3   maritime

4   tropical

 *Discussion*

The "Weather Conditions" column in the chart tells us that the weather in Buffalo was fair. This is the information that suggests what kind of pressure system was over Buffalo. The temperature, though important to the weather, gives us little information about air pressure.

1   Fair weather is usually associated with high pressure systems.

2   Low pressure systems usually bring unstable or rainy conditions.

3   Maritime air masses are associated with oceans. Buffalo, although near Lake Erie, is not near an ocean.

4   Tropical air masses occur near the equator. New York is too far north to be affected directly.

EXAMPLE 5 | Interpreting a Weather Map

According to the map and chart in Example 4, why was it raining in Syracuse?

_____

_____

_____

_____

_____

_____

 **Discussion**

● ●

A front was formed at the boundary between the warm air mass over Albany and the cold air mass over Buffalo. Precipitation usually occurs at such boundaries between air masses.

Base your answers to Examples 6 and 7 on the following weather maps.

EXAMPLE 6 | Movement of Weather Systems

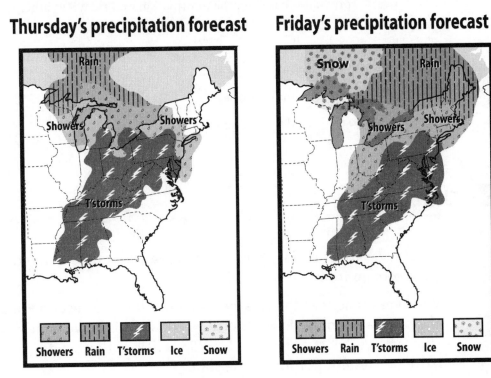

Thursday's precipitation forecast **Friday's precipitation forecast**

Which of the following describes the air mass movement over these two days?

1   east to west

2   west to east

3   stalled over the midwestern United States

4   storms originating in the Gulf of Mexico

Discussion

In North America, as in most of the Northern Hemisphere, the air masses move from west to east, not east to west. These maps show the rain and thunderstorms moving eastward across Indiana, Kentucky, Tennessee, etc., and across the Appalachians to the East Coast.

These maps show movement of air in the midwestern states, not stalling of a weather system. And there are no storms or maritime tropical masses shown in the Gulf of Mexico.

EXAMPLE 7 **Predicting the Weather**

What might a meteorologist predict about Saturday's weather over most of New York State, based on the information on Friday's weather map?

1   fair

2   showers

3   thunderstorms

4   cold with snow

 **Discussion**

1   Saturday will not be fair, because the area will still be covered by the moist air mass coming from the west.

2   We can assume that the weather system will move east on Friday–Saturday about the same amount it did on Thursday–Friday. This movement would still leave showers over most of New York on Saturday, perhaps with some clearing in the extreme western portion of the state.

3   The thunderstorm activity will have moved out to southern New England and the Atlantic Ocean by Saturday.

4   There is no indication on the map of any cold air mass coming down from the north that could turn the rain showers into snow.

Base your answers to Examples 8 through 10 on the contour map below. Points A through F represent locations on the map.

EXAMPLE 8 | **Reading a Contour Map**

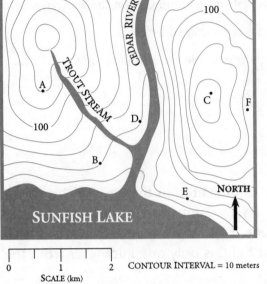

What is the mostly likely elevation of the surface of Sunfish Lake?

1   150 m

2   140 m

3   50 m

4   20 m

 **Discussion**

The key for the map indicates that the contour lines are in intervals of 10 meters. Looking at the map, we see that the contours get larger as they go toward the lake. This means they represent lower elevations as they move down from the steepness of the two hills.

To determine the elevation of Sunfish Lake, start at the 100-meter contour line and subtract 10 meters for every line towards the lake. Or, count the intervals from 100 to the lakeshore. There are 5 intervals.

5 × 10 m = 50 m   100 m − 50 m = 50 m

| EXAMPLE 9 | **Determining Slope on a Contour Map** |

Which statement about hill C is best supported by the map?

1   Hill C is located approximately 2 km west of Cedar River.

2   The steepest slope of hill C is on the western side.

3   Hill C has been shaped by glaciers.

4   The highest possible elevation for hill C is 179 m.

✔ *Discussion*

1   The direction for "North" is indicated in the key for this contour map. If north is at the top of the map, then hill C must be located east of the Cedar River, not west of it. In addition, even if you were confused about the direction, measuring from the scale shows that hill C is only one kilometer from the Cedar River, not two.

2   The steepest slope is on the western side of hill C. On contour maps, a steep slope is indicated by contour lines that are close together, as these are.

3   Hill C was probably not shaped by glaciers, because glacial valleys are usually U-shaped. This valley is steep on one side and gently sloping on the other.

4   The highest elevation for hill C is between 130 and 140 m. Find the 100 m contour line, and add the contour intervals. In this case, the top of Hill C is located higher than three intervals (130 m); there is no fourth interval (140 m).

EXAMPLE 10 | **Reading Elevation**

Which location has the same elevation as location D?

1   A

2   E

3   C

4   F

 *Discussion*

. . . .

1   Location A is 50 m higher than location D.

2   Although it is on the other side of the river, location E is on the same contour line as location D. Therefore it has the same elevation.

3   Location C is across the river and about 70 m higher.

4   Location F, on the other side of the mountain, is about 35 m higher than location D.

EXAMPLE 11 Reading Latitude and Longitude

On the map below, which city or geologic feature is located at 37 degrees North latitude and 120 degrees West longitude?

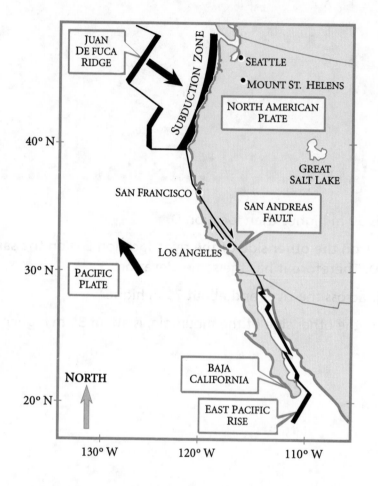

1   Great Salt Lake

2   East Pacific Rise

3   San Francisco

4   Seattle

☑ *Discussion*

Latitude and longitude on a map are read like a graph. For this example, look at the numbers on the left of the map. Find where 37° N would be (between 30° and 40°, marked on the map) and draw a horizontal line to the right. Next, go to the bottom of the map and find 120°W and draw a line upward. Where the two lines intersect is your answer.

1   Great Salt Lake is located at approximately 40° North latitude and 108° West longitude.

2   The East Pacific Rise is located at approximately 20° North latitude and 110° West longitude.

3   San Francisco is located at 37° North latitude and 120° West longitude.

4   Seattle is located at approximately 46° North latitude and 116° West longitude.

EXAMPLE 12 Plate Tectonics

The coastlines of South America and Africa seem to fit together like puzzle pieces. Hundred million-year-old fossils discovered on the two continents are very similar. These two pieces of evidence suggest that

1 ancient animals swam across the Atlantic Ocean

2 volcanic activity joined Africa and South America together

3 Africa and South America were once a single landmass, but broke apart due to continental drift

4 Earth's mantle cooled the landmasses, and they broke apart

 Discussion

1 The Atlantic Ocean is thousands of miles wide. Animals could not have swum across such a great distance. (In any case, the Atlantic Ocean didn't exist 100 million years ago.)

2 Volcanic activity does not join land masses together. In fact, it is often associated with landmasses that are splitting apart.

3 Two hundred million years ago, Africa and South America were still parts of a single world continent that scientists call **Pangaea** (pronounced ***pan-JEE-a***). Then the northern and southern halves of Pangaea split apart. About 120 million years ago, the southern half of Pangaea also started to split apart along the north-south line of the mid-Atlantic Ridge. Convection currents in the Earth's mantle moved the plates apart, carrying the continents of Africa and South America with them. By about 85 million years ago, the split into the American and African tectonic plates was complete, and the Atlantic Ocean was born. Since then, the two continents have been moving steadily apart.

4 The Earth's mantle is hot, not cool. It is so hot that it provides the energy to move the land masses apart in the process called "continental drift."

EXAMPLE 13 Seashells on Mountaintops

Fossils of organisms—seashells, fish, and so on—that lived in shallow sea water have been found in sedimentary rock layers high up in mountain ranges. Earth scientists believe this is evidence that

1   the shallow-water organisms were carried up the mountain by predators

2   fossils were moved by erupting volcanoes

3   ancient rivers flowed away from seas and up into mountains

4   sections of the Earth's crust that were at sea level have changed levels due to folding and faulting

Discussion

1   Predators often do carry their prey to another location to eat it. But it is unlikely that predators would carry their food up a mountain in large enough numbers that scientists would discover fossils of their prey. Also, if the prey were eaten, there would be no remains to form fossils.

2   Molten lava destroys whatever is in its path. That includes fossils. And even if they were not destroyed, they would not be moved up a mountain.

3   The direction of river flow is the result of gravity. Even in ancient times, rivers did not flow uphill.

4   The Earth's crust is broken into large pieces, called **plates**, that are in constant motion. Sometimes, when one plate crashes into another, the rock layers at the area of contact crumple into folds and part of the crust is shoved up into a range of mountains.

Sometimes a plate cracks. This crack is called a **fault**. If the rock on one side of the fault then slides over the rock on the other side, mountains can also be formed.

Scientists infer that the ocean fossils found high in the mountains are there because the seafloor where they once lived was uplifted into mountains by folding and faulting. (One of the first people to figure this out was the famous Renaissance artist and thinker Leonardo da Vinci.)

EXAMPLE 14 Identifying Minerals

On a vacation trip inside an old mine, Judy found an interesting looking mineral. After doing some observations she found the following information: the mineral was shiny and very heavy, it left a black streak on a streak plate, she could scratch it with a coin, and it was not attracted to a magnet.

Using the table below, determine the identity of the mineral.

Name	Hardness	Characteristics	Color	Luster
graphite	2 – 2.5	black streak	silver to grey	metallic
galena	2.5	black streak; very dense and heavy	metallic silver	metallic
biotite mica	2.5 – 3	splits into flexible sheets	black to brown	non-metallic
magnetite	5.5 – 6.5	attracted by magnet; black streak	black to silver	metallic

1   graphite

2   galena

3   biotite mica

4   magnetite

✓ Discussion

Most of the chart is easy to read, but you should know something about the hardness scale to read that part of it.

- Mineral hardness is measured on a scale from 1 to 10.

- Talc, the softest mineral, is a 1; diamond, the hardest, is a 10.

- Your fingernail will scratch anything up to 2.5. A coin will scratch anything up to 3.5. A pocket knife scratches up to 5.5

Since Judy could scratch the mineral with a coin, it must have a hardness of 3.5 or less.

Now let's look at each answer choice:

1   **Graphite** is a mineral form of carbon. One of its uses is in pencil lead. But Judy's mineral can't be graphite. Although graphite is non-magnetic, fairly soft, and shiny like Judy's mineral, it is not very heavy and dense.

2   **Galena** is lead sulfide, a common ore of lead. It has every one of the characteristics of Judy's find. So the find is probably galena.

3   **Biotite mica** is a very common mineral. It is the correct hardness, but it splits into flexible brownish sheets. It is shiny, but its shine is more like glass than like metal. Judy's find is not biotite mica.

4   **Magnetite** has a hardness of 5.5 to 6.5—too hard to be scratched by a coin. And it is attracted by a magnet. So it can't be Judy's find.

EXAMPLE 15 Density

A student wants to rank the following items in order of their densities:

baby oil

a wooden boat

a marble

Describe an investigation that would give the student the necessary information.

_____

_____

_____

_____

_____

_____

☑ Discussion

Here are two approaches that the student could use (there are probably others).

- The student could put the three items in a container of water and see which floated, which partially floated, and which sank. (It would probably be best to put the baby oil in a plastic bag first.)

- A more accurate way would be to use the mathematical formula for density:

$$\text{density} = \frac{\text{mass}}{\text{volume}}$$

First, the student must find the **mass** of each object using a balance (again, it would be best to put the baby oil in a plastic bag; but find the mass of the bag first and subtract its mass from the total of the bag and the baby oil combined).

Next, the student finds the volume of each object. He or she puts each object into a graduated cylinder of water, first making sure that there is no air in the bag of oil. If the object floats, the student uses a straw or something similar to push it all the way under the water. The amount of water displaced would be the volume of the object.

Using the formula above, the student could determine mathematically what the density of each item was, then rank order them.

EXAMPLE 16	**States of Matter**

Complete the table to show the molecular characteristics of three states of matter.

States of matter	Forces between particles	Definite shape	Volume
solid	strong		
liquid	not strong	no	
gas		no	not definite

☑ Discussion

The completed table might look like this:

States of matter	Forces between particles	Definite shape	Volume
solid	strong	yes	definite
liquid	not strong	no	definite
gas	weak	no	not definite

- The forces between particles of a solid are strong, so the solid has a definite shape and volume.

- The forces between the particles of a liquid are not strong, so the liquid takes the shape of the container it is in.

- The forces between the particles of a gas are very weak, so gases do not have a definite volume. They take the shape of the container they are in only if it is closed.

EXAMPLE 17 | **Chemical Change**

Which of the following is an example of something undergoing a chemical change?

1 a melting ice cube

2 a bouncing ball

3 a broken pipe

4 a rusting bike

**Discussion**

1 A melting ice cube is undergoing a physical change, a change from a solid to liquid. This kind of change is called a *phase change* or a change of *state* . It is considered a physical change, not a chemical one, because the water has the same chemical properties as the ice.

2 A bouncing ball is undergoing a change in position as it moves, and a change in shape of the kind known as *elastic deformation*. Both involve changes in energy, but not a chemical change at all.

3 A broken pipe is only the same pipe in smaller pieces.

4 A rusting bike is undergoing a chemical change because oxygen in the air is combining with the iron in the bike to form a new compound, iron oxide. This is a chemical change.

EXAMPLE 18 | Solutions

Observe the physical change shown in the following diagram:

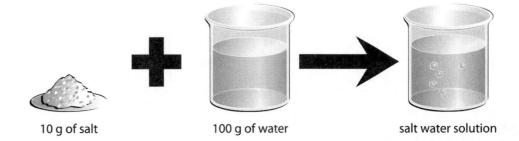

10 g of salt   100 g of water   salt water solution

Notice that the level of water in the beaker is not significantly higher when the salt is added. What is the mass of the salt-water solution?

1   10g

2   100g

3   110g

4   cannot tell from the information given

 *Discussion*

To find the mass of the solution, add the masses of the salt and the water to get 110g. Dissolving salt in water does not add significantly to the volume of the water, but the mass of the two substances does not disappear. Adding 10 grams of salt to 100 grams of water, even though the salt dissolves, still results in 110 grams of salt solution.

EXAMPLE 19 Physical Laws

What scientific principle is being shown in the previous example?

1 The Law of Conservation of Energy

2 Boyle's Law

3 The Salt Hypothesis

4 The Law of Conservation of Mass

 Discussion

1. **The Law of Conservation of Energy** states that in any reaction involving energy, the total amount of energy after the reaction is the same as the total amount of energy before it. This law is not shown by the facts given above (although energy is involved in the dissolving of salt in water).

2. **Boyle's Law** involves gas pressure. Among other things, it states that if you compress a gas in a container to half its size, the gas pressure will double. Boyle's Law has nothing to do with salt solutions.

3 **The Salt Hypothesis** is important in medicine. It states that people who have a high-salt diet tend to have high blood pressure. But it has nothing to do with the mass of a salt solution.

4 **The Law of Conservation of Mass** states that during ordinary chemical and physical changes, matter can neither be created nor destroyed. The total mass of the reactants at the beginning of the reaction equals the total mass of the products at the end. This explains why you only need to add the mass of the salt to the mass of the water to get the mass of the solution.

Originally the laws of Conservation of Energy and Conservation of Mass were quite distinct. But nearly a hundred years ago, Albert Einstein showed that mass could be converted to energy, and vice-versa. As a result, today the laws have become combined into a Law of Conservation of Mass-Energy.

EXAMPLE 20 | Classifying Elements

Elements are made up of atoms. Atoms combine in predictable ways, depending on their characteristics. One model of classification which is used to identify these characteristics is called the

1   Linnaeus method

2   Solubility index

3   Kinetic Energy chart

4   Periodic Table

☑ *Discussion*

● ●

1   **Carolus Linnaeus** was a Swedish botanist who developed a way of classifying plants and animals by their physical characteristics. He did not classify elements, whose existence was unknown when he lived.

2   The **solubility index** of a substance (like salt) is the measure of the amount of the substance that will dissolve in a solvent (like water) at a specific temperature and pressure. It's not a classification of the elements.

3   **Kinetic energy** is the amount of energy an object has because of its motion. Like answer choices 1 and 2, it has nothing to do with classifying the elements.

4   The **Periodic Table** is a way of classifying elements. It was developed by a Russian scientist named Mendeleev. He listed the elements in order by increasing atomic mass. (We now arrange elements by increasing atomic number). He found that he could divide his list into columns so elements with similar properties would align. Scientists use the periodic table to predict how atoms will combine to form molecules and compounds.

EXAMPLE 21 **Non-renewable Resources**

Conservationists urge their neighbors to use renewable resources as sources of energy. Which of the following is a non-renewable resource?

1 wood

2 petroleum

3 wind

4 water power

 **Discussion**

1 Wood is a renewable resource. When forests are harvested, more trees can be planted to replace them. But it takes time for forests to grow. The renewal of the resource is not rapid.

2 Petroleum and petroleum products, like coal and natural gas, come from plant and animal material buried in the earth millions of years ago. Since they take so long to form, they cannot be replaced once they are used. They are non-renewable.

3 Wind is formed by convection currents in the atmosphere created by uneven heating by the sun. The energy from the wind can be used to turn the blades of a windmill. If the windmill is attached to a turbine, which, in turn, is attached to a generator, electricity can be produced. As long as the sun shines, there will be wind. This resource is renewable.

4 Water power is obtained from the kinetic energy of falling water or from water moving forcefully under the pressure of gravity. Water power can generate electricity in much the same way that wind power does. As long as the water supply is renewed by rain, the resource is renewable.

EXAMPLE 22 Refraction

Which of the following diagrams shows refraction of light?

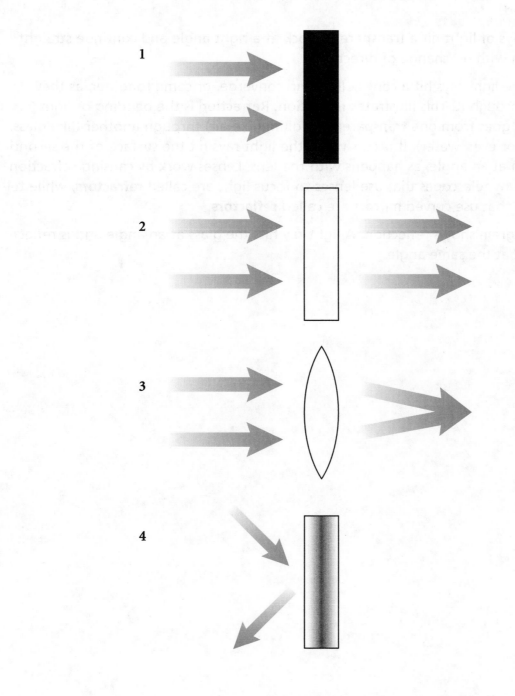

☑ *Discussion*

1   This diagram shows absorption. The light rays hit a black surface and are absorbed.

2   Here, rays of light hit a transparent block at a right angle and continue straight through with no change of direction.

3   Here, the light rays hit a convex lens and converge, or come together, as they move through it. This illustrates refraction. Refraction is the bending of light when it goes from one transparent medium (like air) through another (like glass, plastic, or even water). It occurs when the light rays hit the surface of the second medium at an angle, as happens with the lens. Lenses work by causing refraction This is why telescopes that use lenses to focus light are called **refractors**, while telescopes that use curved mirrors are called **reflectors**.

4   This diagram shows reflection. A light ray hits the glass at an angle and is reflected back at the same angle.

| EXAMPLE 23 | Conductors and Insulators |

Joe wanted to determine which objects listed on the chart below were good conductors of electricity. He set up an experimental apparatus as shown in the following diagram:

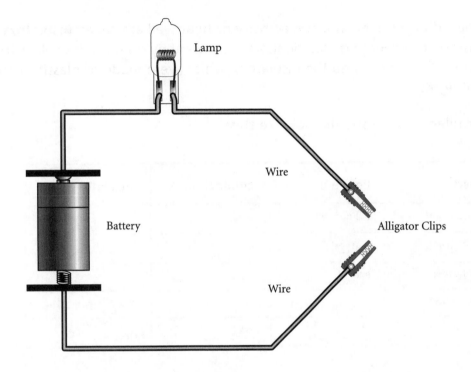

Joe attached the alligator clips to each of the objects he was testing to see if they conducted electricity or not. Complete the data table below, based on the partial information Joe supplied.

object	light bulb	conductor	insulator
plastic spoon	did not light		
copper penny		yes	no
metal paper clip	bulb lit		no
rubber eraser			yes
aluminum rod	yes	yes	

☑ Discussion

Materials that allow electricity (or heat) to flow through them are called **conductors**. Good conductors are usually made of metal, especially silver, copper, and aluminum. In Joe's experiment, conductors caused the bulb to light.

Materials that do not conduct electricity or heat well are called **insulators**. Insulators are very useful in preventing electric shock because they do not allow electricity to pass through. When Joe tested the insulators, which were made of plastic or rubber, the bulb did not light.

So the filled in chart should look like this:

object	light bulb	conductor	insulator
plastic spoon	did not light	no	yes
copper penny	bulb lit	yes	no
metal paper clip	bulb lit	yes	no
rubber eraser	did not light	no	yes
aluminum rod	yes	yes	no

EXAMPLE 24 **Friction**

The librarian was pushing a box full of books through the school. Which surface would be hardest to move the box across?

1   the gym floor

2   the tiled hallway floor

3   the carpeted library floor

4   the vinyl cafeteria floor

 **Discussion**

The hard, waxed surface of the gym floor, the tiled hallway floor, and the vinyl cafeteria floor would all allow the box to slide easily. There would be very little friction with the box on these surfaces.

But the rough carpeting in the library would create more frictional drag on the box and make it harder to push.

EXAMPLE 25 **Simple Machines**

There are many examples of simple machines in nature. What kind of simple machine is shown in the following diagram of a person's arm?

1   a lever

2   an inclined plane

3   a battery

4   a ramp

✓ Discussion

1   A simple machine is a device that changes the size or direction of a force. A **lever** is a simple machine that consists of a bar and a pivot point, or **fulcrum**. The arm shown here is like a bar with the elbow acting as the fulcrum.

2   An **inclined plane** is usually a plank of some sort. It makes work easier because objects can be slid or rolled up the plank rather than lifted straight up. The arm shown here is not acting as an inclined plane.

3   A **battery** is an electrochemical cell that transforms chemical energy into electrical energy. It is not a simple machine.

4. A **ramp** is just another name for an inclined plane. It is a simple machine, but it is not the one shown here.

Other simple machines are the wheel and axle, the pulley, the wedge, and the screw.

NEW YORK STATE INTERMEDIATE LEVEL SCIENCE
Practice Test 1

Part A *Directions (1 – 17): Each question is followed by four choices. Decide which choice is the best answer. Mark your answer in the spaces provided on the separate answer sheet by writing the number of the answer you have chosen.*

1   Which part of a cell allows nutrients and other materials to enter or leave the cell?

   1 cytoplasm
   2 nucleus
   3 chloroplast
   4 cell membrane

2   Which human body system controls production of the hormones that regulate body functions?

   1 digestive
   2 endocrine
   3 respiratory
   4 skeletal

3   Hereditary information is found in a cell's

   1 chloroplasts
   2 chromosomes
   3 cytoplasm
   4 membranes

4   What is a major cause of variation within a species?

   1 sexual reproduction
   2 asexual reproduction
   3 extinction
   4 photosynthesis

5   Which process is shown in the diagram below?

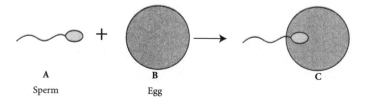

   1 metamorphosis
   2 regulation
   3 fertilization
   4 respiration

6   A male chimpanzee has 48 chromosomes in each of his regular body cells. How many chromosomes would be found in each of his sperm cells?

   1 96
   2 8
   3 24
   4 12

7   The diagram below shows materials needed for survival being transported inside a plant.

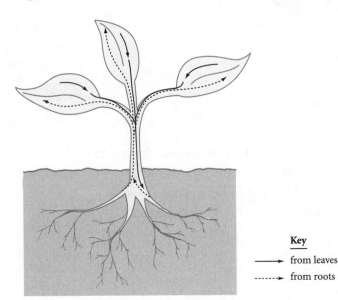

Key
→ from leaves
⤍ from roots

   Which body system performs this function in humans?

   1 circulatory system
   2 digestive system
   3 excretory system
   4 respiratory system

8   The energy content of food is measured in

   1 ounces
   2 degrees
   3 grams
   4 Calories

9   The diagram below shows the Moon revolving around Earth as viewed from space.

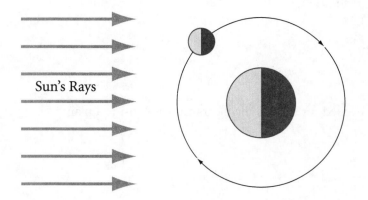

What makes it possible to see the Moon from Earth?

1 The surface of the Moon emits its own light, which can be seen from Earth.
2 The Moon absorbs light during the day and emits the light at night.
3 Light emitted by Earth illuminates the Moon's surface, making it visible.
4 Light emitted by the Sun is reflected to Earth by the Moon's surface.

10   The solid part of the Earth's surface is called the

1 hydrosphere
2 lithosphere
3 troposphere
4 atmosphere

11   A rock that contains fossil seashells was most likely formed as a result of

1 volcanic activity
2 sedimentation
3 heat and pressure
4 magma cooling

12   The diagram below shows the rock cycle.

Which two processes result in the formation of igneous rocks?

1 melting and solidification
2 sedimentation and evaporation
3 crystallization and cementation
4 compression and precipitation

13   The cartoon below shows a humorous view of a scientific phenomenon.

What process is occurring that makes the child's breath become visible?

1 boiling
2 melting
3 condensation
4 evaporation

14   In which situation is a chemical reaction occurring?

   1   salt dissolves in water
   2   a nail rusts
   3   ice melts
   4   a glass breaks

15   As ice cream melts, its molecules

   1   absorb heat energy and move farther apart
   2   absorb heat energy and move closer together
   3   release heat energy and move farther apart
   4   release heat energy and move closer together

16   Which diagram best shows the property of refraction?

(1)

(3)

(2)

(4)

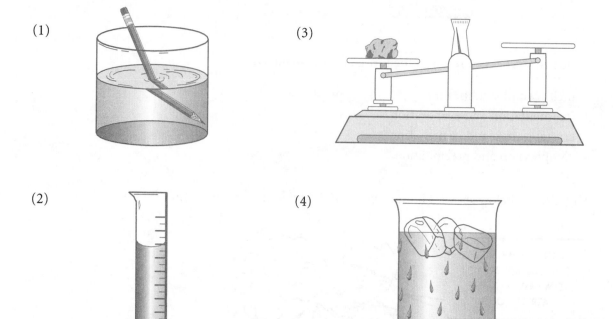

17   A student pushes against a wall with 20 N of force and the wall does not move. In this situation, the wall exerts

   1   0 N of force
   2   less than 20 N of force
   3   20 N of force
   4   more than 20 N of force

Part B *Directions (18 – 34): Each question is followed by four choices. Decide which choice is the best answer. Mark your answer in the spaces provided on the separate answer sheet by writing the number of the answer you have chosen.*

18 The data table below shows the average distance of four planets from the Sun and the approximate time it takes those planets to orbit the sun.

Planet	Average Distance from the Sun (millions of kilometers)	Approximate Time It Takes the Planet to Orbit the Sun (Earth days)
Mercury	57.9	88
Venus	108.2	225
Earth	149.6	365
Mars	227.9	687

Which statement is best supported by the data in the table?

1 Venus takes less time to orbit the Sun than Mercury does.
2 Mars takes less time to orbit the Sun than Earth does.
3 Mars takes more time to orbit the Sun than Earth does.
4 Venus takes more time to orbit the Sun than Mars does.

19 The data table below shows the masses and volumes of three objects (A, B, and C).

A	B	C
Mass = 4 g	Mass = 6 g	Mass = 8 g
Volume = 2 cm^3	Volume = 6 cm^3	Volume = 4 cm^3

The formula for calculating an object's density is: Density = $\frac{\text{Mass}}{\text{Volume}}$.

Which statement about the densities of these three objects is correct?

1 B is more dense than A.
2 A is more dense than C.
3 B and C have equal densities.
4 A and C have equal densities.

20   The diagram below shows the frequency and wavelength of various types of electromagnetic energy.

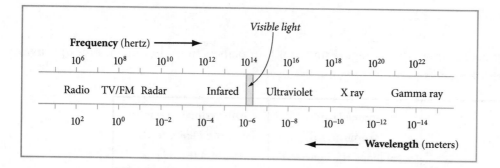

Which type of electromagnetic wave has a wavelength of approximately 10^{-10} meter and a frequency of 10^{18} hertz?

1 infrared
2 radio
3 X ray
4 radar

21   The graph below shows the distance and time traveled by four cars.

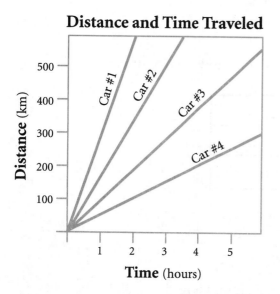

Which car traveled the slowest?

1 Car #1
2 Car #2
3 Car #3
4 Car #4

Photocopying any part of this book is prohibited by law.

Directions (22 – 34): For each question, write your answer in the spaces provided.

Base your answers to questions 22 through 24 on the diagrams and data table below.

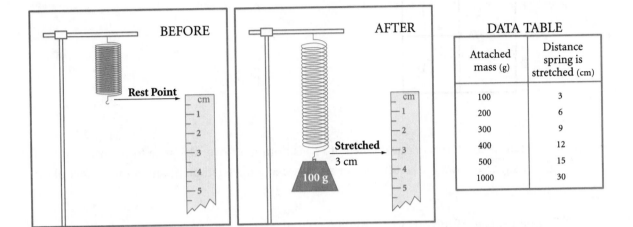

Attached mass (g)	Distance spring is stretched (cm)
100	3
200	6
300	9
400	12
500	15
1000	30

22 State the relationship between the mass attached to the end of the spring and the length the spring is stretched.

_____

_____

_____

_____

_____

23 Predict how many centimeters the spring will stretch if a total mass of 700 grams were attached.

_____

_____

_____

_____

24 What mass would be needed to stretch the spring to a length of 60 cm?

_____

_____

_____

_____

Base your answers to questions 25 through 27 on the Punnett square and information below.

	T	T
t	Tt	Tt
t	Tt	Tt

In a certain plant, the gene for tall height (T) is dominant over the gene for short height (t). The Punnett square shows the results of a cross between a pure tall plant and a pure short plant.

25 What percentage of the offspring would be tall plants?

_____

26 Use the Punnett square below to show the results of crossing two of the offspring shown in the Punnett square above.

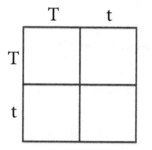

	T	t
T		
t		

27 Which process is represented by the use of the Punnett square?

1 natural selection
2 sexual reproduction
3 pollination
4 mutation

Base your answers to questions 28 through 32 on the food web shown below.

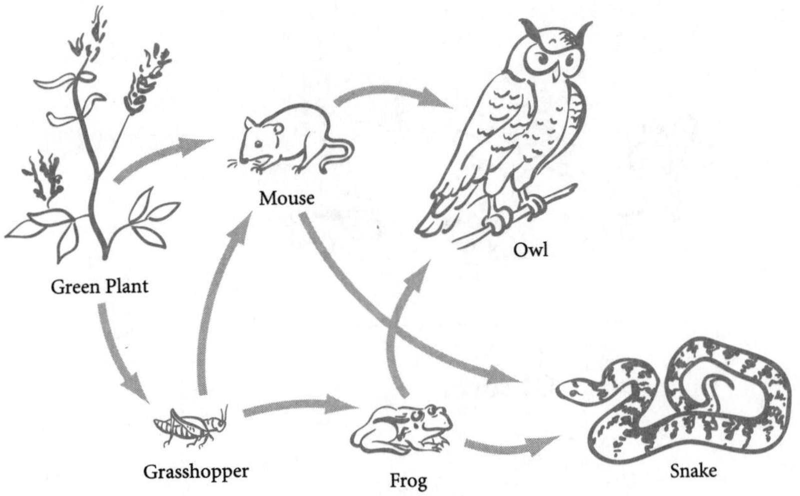

28   Identify a producer in this food web.

_____

29   Identify an herbivore in this food web.

_____

30   Identify a carnivore in this food web.

_____

31   Identify an omnivore in this food web.

_____

32   Explain why removing the snake from this food web might result in a decrease in the grasshopper population.

_____

_____

_____

_____

Base your answers to questions 33 and 34 on the diagram below, which shows a form of reproduction.

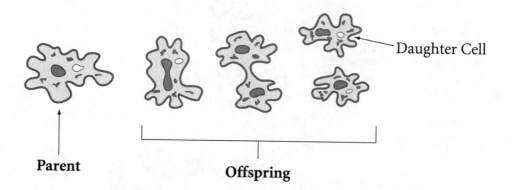

Parent   **Offspring**   Daughter Cell

33   Which type of reproduction is shown in the diagram?

_____

34   How does the genetic material of the daughter cell compare to the genetic material of the parent cell?

_____

_____

Part C *Directions (35 – 45): For each question, write your answer in the space provided.*

Base your answers to questions 35 and 36 on the charts below, which show two elements (iron and sulfur) and their properties. The arrows indicate that these elements may combine to form either a mixture of iron and sulfur or the compound iron sulfide.

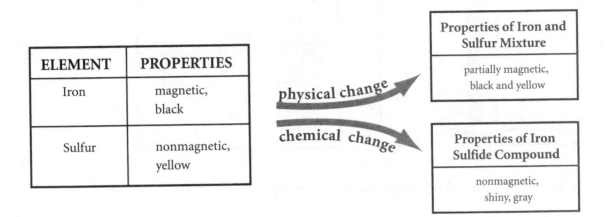

ELEMENT	PROPERTIES
Iron	magnetic, black
Sulfur	nonmagnetic, yellow

Properties of Iron and Sulfur Mixture

partially magnetic, black and yellow

Properties of Iron Sulfide Compound

nonmagnetic, shiny, gray

physical change

chemical change

35   How could a student use a magnet to indicate that combining iron and sulfur to produce the mixture of iron and sulfur is a physical change?

_____

_____

_____

36   What evidence indicates that a chemical change took place when the iron and sulfur combined to form iron sulfide?

_____

_____

_____

Base your answers to questions 37 and 38 on the diagrams below, which show two situations in which energy transformations are occurring.

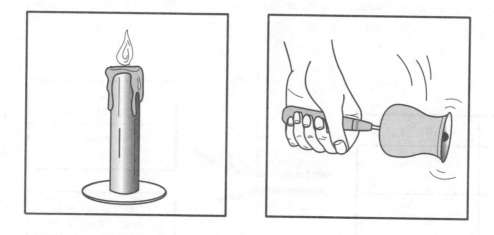

37   As the candle burns, which energy transformation occurs?

_____

_____

38   As the bell rings, which energy transformation occurs?

_____

_____

39   A student plays tennis several times a week. She notices that the tennis ball seems to bounce higher on some courts than on other courts. She wonders if this has something to do with the surface of the court. Design an experiment to see if her hypothesis is correct. Include these elements in your response:

- State the hypothesis.
- Identify the factor to be varied.
- Identify two factors that should be held constant.
- Clearly describe the procedures.

_____

_____

_____

_____

_____

_____

_____

_____

_____

_____

_____

_____

_____

_____

Base your answers to questions 40 through 42 on the graphs below, which show the laboratory growth of two microorganisms when provided with adequate food and grown in **separate test tubes.**

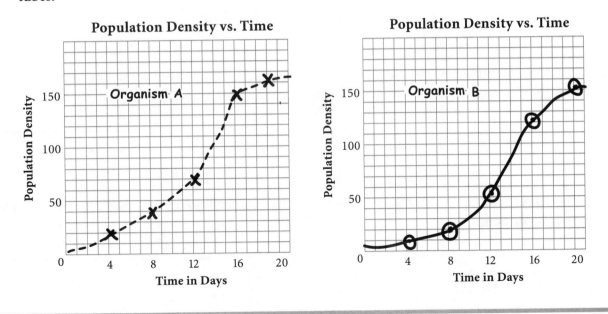

40   The data below were obtained when organism A and organism B were grown with adequate food in the **same test tube**.

Population Density	Day					
	0	4	8	12	16	20
Organism A	5	50	100	75	25	10
Organism B	5	25	75	125	150	125

On the grid below, make a graph of the data from the table above according to the instructions below.

a Place an X to show the population of organism A for each interval in the 20-day period.
b Connect the X's with a dashed line. Make a key that indicates this line represents the data for organism A.
c Place a dot in a circle to show the population of organism B for each interval in the 20-day period.
d Connect circled dots with a solid line. Make a key that indicates this line represents the data for organism B.

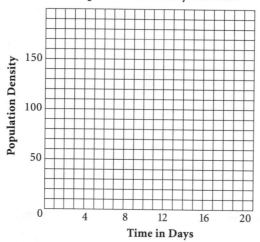

Population Density vs. Time

41   State a relationship that may have produced the results shown when organism A and organism B were grown together. Explain your answer, using the graphed data.

_____

_____

42   Based on your graph, predict the population density of organism A or organism B at day 21. Explain your prediction.

_____

_____

Base your answers to questions 43 through 45 on the information below and on your knowledge of science. The page of notes shown below was made by a student doing a research project about hail.

Some Observations about Hail:

1   Hailstones are fairly round in shape.
2   When cut in half or held up to the light, layers can be seen in the hailstone.
3   Average diameter of hailstones found after last summer's storms:
    July 12 - 6 mm
    July 26 - 9 mm
    August 12 - 20 mm
    August 26 - 12 mm

Background Information Found in Science Book:

1   The precipitation dropped during a hailstorm is called hailstones.
2   Hail causes damage to crops, buildings, and vehicles.
3   Hailstones are usually more than 5 mm in diameter.
4   Thunderstorms form from tall clouds which have temperatures below 0°C in their upper regions. They have strong updrafts pushing the air toward the top.
5   The layers in a hailstone are caused by the path the hail takes as it falls.
6   A new layer forms each time the hailstone is pushed into the freezing zone.

43   On the diagram below, draw a path that would produce a hailstone that has three layers. You can
      practice on a separate sheet. Be sure your path starts and finishes at the points shown. The dotted
      line separates the thunderstorm into Zone A, which is above 0°C, and Zone B, which is below 0°C.
      When you are satisfied with your path, copy it onto the diagram on your answer sheet. Your answer
      will be evaluated by how well the path you have drawn could produce a three-layer hailstone.

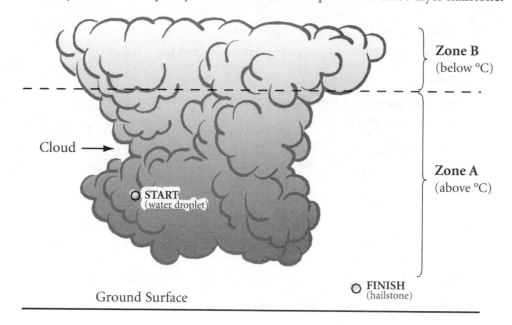

44   Based on the student's observations above, which of last summer's storms most likely had the
      strongest updrafts associated with it? Give two reasons to support your answer.

      _____

      _____

      _____

      _____

      _____

45   Based on the background information in the student's notes on the previous page, identify one
      problem that can be caused by hailstorms.

      _____

      _____

      _____

      _____

Part A

1. *The correct answer is 4, cell membrane.*

   1 **Cytoplasm** is the material in the cell between the cell membrane and the nucleus.
   2 The **nucleus** is the part of the cell that contains the cell's genetic material, DNA.
   3 **Chloroplasts** are organelles that contain chlorophyll. They are found only in the cells of plants and other eukaryotes that are capable of photosynthesis. Chloroplasts are the sites where photosynthesis take place.
   4 The **cell membrane** is an organelle that surrounds the cytoplasm of the cell. Nutrients, wastes, and other materials move in and out of the cell through the cell membrane by the process of diffusion. In diffusion, materials move through the cell membrane from the region of higher concentration to the region of lower concentration, so that the concentration on either side of the membrane tends to equalize.

2. *The correct answer is 2, endocrine.*

   1 The **digestive system** does not control hormones. It is made up of the organs that break food down into less complex molecules
   2 **The endocrine system** includes organs called glands that send chemicals (hormones) into the blood stream to regulate growth and body functions.
   3 The **respiratory system** is made up of the organs that bring oxygen into the body and release carbon dioxide from the body (gas exchange).
   4 The **skeletal system** consists of bones that, together with muscles, allow the body to move to escape danger, obtain food and shelter, and reproduce.

3. *The correct answer is 2, chromosomes.*

   1 **Chloroplasts** contain chlorophyll and are the sites of photosynthesis.
   2 **Chromosomes** are threadlike structures that contain DNA, the genetic material. They are found in a cell's nucleus, and they carry the cell's hereditary information.
   3 **Cytoplasm** is the material in the cell between the nucleus and the cell membrane.
   4 **Membranes** are organelles that surround the cytoplasm of the cell. They regulate movement of material into and out of the cells.

4.   *The correct answer is 1, sexual reproduction.*

1 **During sexual reproduction**, half of the genes come from each parent, genes are paired, and the dominant one is expressed—that is, it shows up in the offspring. As a result, the offspring is not identical to either parent. This is a major cause of variation within a species.

2 In **asexual reproduction**, all the genes come from a single parent, so the offspring is identical to that parent.

3 **Extinction** occurs when no more individuals of a species exist. It does not cause variation within a species.

4 **Photosynthesis** is the process green plants use to make food. It has nothing to do with variation within a species.

5.   *The correct answer is 3, fertilization.*

1 **Metamorphosis** is a multi-step process that some organisms undergo as they move from a larval stage to an adult. One example of metamorphosis is the change of a caterpillar to a butterfly or moth. So is the change from a tadpole to a frog.

2 **Regulation** is the interaction of the nervous and endocrine systems. This process is necessary for an organism to maintain homeostasis—internal balance.

3 **Fertilization** is the process of male sperm (A) joining with a female egg (B) to form a **zygote** (C)—a fertilized egg.

4 **Respiration** is a process in which cells use oxygen to release the energy stored in food. Carbon dioxide is released during this process. The term respiration is also used for the act of breathing. But neither process is shown in the diagram.

6.   *The correct answer is 3, 24 chromosomes.*

Sperm (and egg) cells are produced by a special form of cell division called **meiosis**. Meiosis occurs only in the sex cells of organisms. It results in daughter cells with only half the number of chromosomes that the organism has in its regular body cells—muscle cells, for example. A male chimpanzee's sperm cells therefore would have 24 chromosomes—half the number (48) of his body cells. (And a female chimpanzee would have the same number of chromosomes—24—in her egg cells.)

During sexual reproduction, the full number of 48 chromosomes is restored—24 from the mother chimpanzee and 24 from the father chimpanzee (24 + 24 = 48).

7.   *The correct answer is 1, circulatory.*

1   This diagram of a plant shows materials being transported around the plant (like water and nutrients from the roots) to enable photosynthesis to occur. The similar transport system in humans is the **circulatory system**. It is made up of the heart, the blood, and the blood vessels that move substances around the body to the cells.

2   In humans, the **digestive system** is responsible for the mechanical and chemical breakdown of food. It is not a transport system that extends to all parts of the body.

3   The **excretory system** is responsible for the disposal of dissolved waste molecules, elimination of liquid and gaseous wastes, and the removal of excess heat energy.

4   The **respiratory system** supplies oxygen to the cells to release energy stored in food and removes carbon dioxide (gas exchange).

8.   *The correct answer is 4, Calories.*

1   **Ounces** is a unit of mass and of weight in the English system of measurement.

2   **Degrees** is a measure of temperature.

3   **Grams** is a unit of mass and of weight in the metric system of measurement.

4   **Calories** are a measure of the energy content of food. A calorie (with a small letter) is a measure of the amount of heat energy necessary to raise one gram of water one degree Celsius. It is a very small amount of heat energy, so when measuring the energy content of food, scientists prefer to use a unit called a kilocalorie—1000 calories. For short, this 1000-calorie unit is also called a Calorie, but the word is capitalized.

9.   *The correct answer is 4, light emitted by the Sun is reflected to Earth by the Moon's surface.*

1   The Moon does not produce any light of its own.

2   The Moon does not absorb light during the day and emit it at night. It reflects sunlight in the daytime too, but it is easier to see the moon against the night sky. But you have probably seen the Moon during the day.

3   Earth does not emit light either, so it cannot illuminate the Moon's surface.

4. We see the Moon because sunlight lights it—the same way sunlight lights objects on Earth. This is what the diagram shows.

10.   *The correct answer is 2, lithosphere.*

1   The **hydrosphere** is liquid, not solid. It is the part of the Earth which is water, both on the surface and below. It includes the ocean, lakes and rivers, and underground water.

2   The **lithosphere** is the outer solid shell of the Earth. It is composed of the crust and the solid part of the layer under the crust, the mantle.

3 The **troposphere** is gaseous, not solid. It is the layer of the atmosphere closest to the Earth's surface.

4 The **atmosphere** is the blanket of gases that surround the Earth.

11. *The correct answer is 2, sedimentation.*

1 **Volcanic activity** produces lava (liquid rock that flows out of a volcano). When lava cools, it makes an igneous rock. But during its liquid phase, this material is so hot that it destroys any fossils it touches. You won't find any fossils in igneous rock.

2 **Sedimentation** occurs when particles of rock and soil are carried along by water or wind. These particles are deposited on top of one another and become cemented together to form **sedimentary rock**. In the process they often trap seashells, the bones of animals, and sometimes even plant material in the layers. If conditions are right, these organic remains can then become fossilized. Nearly all fossils are found in sedimentary rock.

3 When great **heat and pressure** are applied to rocks, they change form. The new rocks are called metamorphic rocks, and they usually have new physical and chemical properties. But the heat and pressure that form metamorphic rocks are almost always enough to destroy any fossils that might have been in the original rock.

4 **Magma** is underground melted rock. It may burst out of a volcano as lava, or **magma cooling** may slowly take place underground to form bodies of igneous rock like granite. Magma has a temperature of hundreds or even thousands of degrees Celsius. The process of melting rock to form magma is enough to destroy any fossils that might have been in the parent rock.

12. *The correct answer is 1, melting and solidification.*

The rock cycle is a process in nature during which rocks are continually changing form over long periods of time. To answer this question, you should study the diagram and note the direction of the arrows. Since the question asks you about the formation of igneous rock, find that box at the top of the diagram. Then find the arrows that point to it, and work from there.

1 An arrow from *solidification* points to the *igneous rock* box, and an arrow from *melting* points to the *solidification* box. So the diagram shows that igneous rocks form by **melting and solidification**. First, other rocks melt, and then the melt solidifies by cooling.

2 **Sedimentation** is part of the process of forming sedimentary rocks, but **evaporation** has nothing to do with rock formation. The diagram shows that all kinds of rock are weathered and eroded, then deposited to form sediments. These sediments are buried and cemented together to form sedimentary rock, pictured at the bottom of the diagram.

3. **Crystallization and cementation** are both important rock-forming processes, even though they are not shown on the diagram. But only crystallization is involved in forming igneous rock. The minerals in the molten rock form crystals as the rock cools and solidifies. (Crystallization is also important in forming metamorphic rock, where crystals of new minerals are formed from older rock by heat and pressure.)

Cementation is not part of making an igneous rock. It occurs during the formation of sedimentary rock, when dissolved minerals are deposited between the particles of sediment, cementing them together into rock.

4. **Compression** takes place when pressure forms metamorphic rock. It is not important in the formation of igneous rock from melted rock. **Precipitation** usually refers to rain and snow—which have nothing to do with rock formation.

Here's the most important thing to notice: *You don't need all this information to answer the question.* Only the words **melting and solidification** are shown on the diagram. So they are probably the correct answer.

13. *The correct answer is 3, condensation.*

   1 **Boiling** occurs when a liquid changes to a gas.
   2 **Melting** occurs when a solid changes to a liquid.

   3 **Condensation** is the process where water vapor is changed into liquid water. The child can see his breath because his breath is warm and the air is cold. When the water vapor in his breath is cooled, water droplets are formed in the air. These droplets reflect and scatter light, and the child's breath is visible as a white mist.

   4 **Evaporation** occurs when a liquid changes to a gas.

14. *The correct answer is 2, a nail rusts.*

   1 **Salt dissolves in water**; however, no changes in chemical properties have taken place. If the water evaporated, the salt would be left behind, and it would have the same chemical properties as the original salt.

   2 When a **nail rusts**, a chemical reaction is occurring. In a chemical reaction, substances react with each other in characteristic ways to form new substances with different chemical and physical properties. When **a nail rusts**, the iron in the nail combines with the oxygen in the air. It forms a new substance, the reddish form of iron oxide we call rust.

   3 **Ice melts** to form water. This process is only a phase change. No chemical properties have changed. Melting is considered a physical change, not a chemical one.

   4 When **a glass breaks**, it still has all the properties of the original glass, except in smaller pieces.

15. *The correct answer is 1, absorb heat energy and move farther apart.*

   Heat moves in predictable ways. It always moves from warmer objects to cooler ones. The ice cream would **absorb heat energy** from the surrounding air until both the ice cream and the air reached the same temperature.

   The absorption of heat energy makes molecules **move farther apart**. Eventually, if enough heat energy is absorbed, a solid is transformed into a liquid. and the ice cream melts. (Molecules moving even farther apart can transform a liquid into a gas, but ice cream doesn't get that hot in the air.) When ice cream freezes, the opposite happens. The molecules release heat energy and move closer together.

16. *The correct answer is 1, the picture of the pencil in the beaker of water.*

1 When light energy, which allows us to see the pencil, moves from one transparent medium to another, it changes speed. As it changes speed, it also changes direction. In this example, the light changes speed as it moves from the air to the water. When it enters the water it also changes direction, so the pencil appears bent.

2 Picture 2 shows a graduated cylinder with a **meniscus**, a dip in the surface of a liquid. The formation of a meniscus is a result of surface tension. It has nothing to do with refraction.

3 Picture 3 shows a double pan balance being used to measure the mass of an object. Measuring mass is not involved in refraction.

4 Picture 4 shows condensation occurring on a beaker of ice water, as the water vapor in the air next to the beaker cools and changes to liquid water droplets.

17. *The correct answer is 3, 20 N of force.*

1 Force is measured in newtons (N). If the wall exerted 0 N of force when the student pushed it, it would have moved, fallen down, or been pushed over. Motion occurs when forces on objects are not in balance.

2. The same thing would have happened if the wall exerted less than 20 N of force against the student's push of 20 N.

3 In this case, the wall did not move, so equal forces were being exerted. If the student pushed against the wall with 20 N of force, and no movement occurred, the wall must have been pushing back with an equal amount of force—in this example, 20 N.

4. If the wall had been exerting more than 20 N, the student would have been pushed back.

Part B

18. ***The correct answer is 3, Mars takes more time to orbit the Sun than Earth does.***

To answer this question, you should read each answer choice and check it against the information on the data table. For example:

1 The table indicates that Venus takes 225 Earth days to orbit the Sun and Mercury takes 88 days. So Statement #1 "Venus takes less time to orbit the Sun than Mercury does" is incorrect.

2 The table indicates that Mars takes 687 Earth days to orbit the Sun and Earth only takes 365 days. So the statement "Mars takes less time to orbit the sun than Earth does" is also incorrect

3 The table indicates that Mars takes 687 Earth days to orbit the Sun and Earth takes 365 days. So Statement #3 "Mars takes more time to orbit the Sun than Earth does" is correct.

4 Venus takes 225 Earth days to orbit the Sun and Mars takes 687 days, so Statement #4 "Venus takes more time to orbit the Sun than Mars does" is incorrect.

Notice that you don't need all the information in the table to answer the question! Although this chart also indicates "average distance from the Sun," don't be confused by this information. Question 18 is only asking about the comparison of the times it takes planets to orbit the Sun.

19. ***The correct answer is 4, A and C have equal densities.***

Scientists often use mathematical formulas. This question is asking you to use the density formula to calculate the density for 3 objects and compare your results. Using the data given and the formula

$$\text{Density} = \frac{\text{Mass}}{\text{Volume}}$$

you will find the following:

Object A	$\text{Density} = \dfrac{4g}{2cm^3}$	$= \dfrac{2g}{cm^3}$
Object B	$\text{Density} = \dfrac{6g}{6cm^3}$	$= \dfrac{1g}{cm^3}$
Object C	$\text{Density} = \dfrac{8g}{4cm^3}$	$= \dfrac{2g}{cm^3}$

Using these results, look at the answer choices.

1 "B is more dense than A."

   B's density is $\frac{1g}{cm^3}$, and A's is $\frac{2g}{cm^3}$.

   Therefore, B is less dense than A, so this statement is incorrect

2 "A is more dense than C."

   A's density is $\frac{2g}{cm^3}$, and C's is also $\frac{2g}{cm^3}$.

   The densities of both objects are equal, so this statement is incorrect.

3 "B and C have equal densities."

   B's density is $\frac{1g}{cm^3}$, and C's is $\frac{2g}{cm^3}$.

   Therefore, C is more dense than B, so this statement is incorrect.

4 "A and C have equal densities."

   A's density is $\frac{2g}{cm^3}$, and C's is also $\frac{2g}{cm^3}$.

   The densities of the two objects are equal, so this statement is correct.

20. *The correct answer is 3, x-ray.*

Electromagnetic energy is measured in both frequency (hertz) and wavelength. The **wavelength** is the distance from the peak of one wave to the peak of the next. The **frequency** is the number of waves that pass a given point in one second.

High-energy waves have their wave peaks much closer together than low energy waves. Therefore, the higher the energy of a wave, the less distance there is between wave peaks. This means that high-energy waves have low (short) wavelengths.

And these high-energy waves, with close-together peaks, will have a high frequency. More peaks will pass a given point in a second, since all electromagnetic waves travel at the same speed, no matter what their energy.

This diagram is really the two scales put together (frequency, measured in hertz, and wavelength, measured in meters). Look at each of the answer choices and find it on the diagram. Look above and below the word at the scales to determine the frequency and wavelength.

1 Infrared is near the middle of the spectrum with a frequency of 10^{12} hertz and a wavelength of 10^{-4} meters. This answer is, therefore, incorrect.

2 Radio is at the extreme left of the spectrum with a frequency of 10^6 hertz and a wavelength of 10^2 meters. So this answer is also incorrect.

3 X-rays fall into the range of electromagnetic energy that has a wavelength of 10^{-10} meters and a frequency of 10^{18} hertz. So this is the correct answer.

4 Radar is between TV/FM and infrared rays, with a frequency of approximately 10^9 hertz and 10^{-1} meters. So it is incorrect, too.

Notice that you can easily answer the question without a deep understanding of electromagnetic waves. If you can find the words X ray on the diagram, you can also find the numbers 10^{18} and 10^{-10} above and below it.

21. ***The correct answer is 4, Car #4.***

This question tests whether you know how to get information from a line graph.

The graph shows the distance (km) each car traveled over a period of several hours. To answer the question "which car traveled slowest?" you could start with a time—say, five hours—and find the approximate distance each car traveled in that time. The car that covers the least distance in 5 hours is the slowest.

First, find 5 hours at the bottom of the chart. Then move up to the first line you come to—Car # 4. From there, move left. You'll see that Car #4 travels about between 200 and 300 km in 5 hours. Then do the same for the other cars.

1 Car #1 – over 500 km in 5 hours. In fact, it travels 500 km in about 2 hours
2 Car #2 – also over 500 km in 5 hours. in fact, it travels 500 km in a little over 3 hours
3 Car #3 – a little less than 500 km in 5 hours
4 Car #4 – only about 275 miles in 5 hours

Another way to solve the problem is to look at the slope of the lines. The line with the steepest slope belongs to the fastest car, and vice versa. So Car #4 is the slowest. It has the flattest slope.

Questions 22-24

Use the diagrams to help you visualize this experimental set-up. Use the data table to obtain your answers. You can see that for a 100 g mass, the spring stretched 3 cm. According to the data table, for every 100 grams added to the spring, it stretched another 3 cm.

22. ***Your answer might say something like any of the following:***

• The more mass you add, the longer the spring gets.
• The spring gets longer as the mass increases; they are dependent on one another.
• There is a direct relationship between the mass and the stretch of the spring.
• The length that the spring is stretched is directly proportional to the weight of the attached mass.

The best answer would express the quantitative relationship between the mass and the stretch of the spring:

- The relationship between the mass and the length that the spring is stretched is given by the formula $s = \frac{3m}{100}$, where s is the length (in cm) that the spring is stretched and m is the mass (in grams) attached to the spring.

All the bulleted answers are correct, but some are better than others. They are listed roughly in ascending order, from the least to the most complete. The last answer would probably receive the highest score.

23. ***The spring will stretch 21 cm if 700 grams are attached.***

The distance increases 3 cm for every 100 grams that is attached, based on the pattern established or on the equation $s = \frac{3m}{100}$.

You could also get the answer by expanding the data table:

500 g	15 cm
600 g	18 cm
700 g	21 cm
800 g	24 cm
900 g	27 cm
1000 g	30 cm

The expanded table shows that if 700 g were attached, the spring would stretch 21 cm.

24. ***The answer is 2,000 grams.***

The data table shows 30 cm for 1000 grams of mass, so if the distance is doubled (60 cm), the mass must double (2000 g) as well.

Questions 25-27

Punnett squares are a way to diagram genetic combinations that may result in offspring produced by sexual reproduction. This Punnett square shows the result of a genetic cross between pure tall (T) plants and pure short (t) plants where tall is dominant.

25. ***100% of the plants would be tall.***

Each offspring's genotype, as shown in the Punnett square, is Tt. T is dominant, so all plants would be tall. The recessive gene t would not be expressed in the offspring.

26. ***The second generation crossing will result in three T (tall) plants for every t (short) plant.***

The question asks for the results of the crossing of two of the first-generation offspring shown in the Punnett square—that is, the crossing of Tt with another Tt.

To answer the question, construct a second Punnett square for the cross of Tt and Tt. The boxes of the square show the results of this new, second-generation crossing:

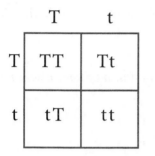

There are 3 offspring with at least one T in their genotype, and only 1 offspring (tt) with no T. So the second generation crossing will result in 3 T (tall) plants for every t (short) plant.

27. ***The correct answer is 2, sexual reproduction.***

1 **Natural selection** is the process where organisms that are better adapted to an environment thrive and produce offspring with the same qualities. Natural selection might act on the offspring produced in the proportions shown in the Punnett square—for example, short plants might die before they can produce offspring—but the square itself does not show the process of natural selection.

2 **Sexual reproduction** is the process by which offspring receive one set of genes from the mother and one set from the father. The Punnett square shows all possible results of the combination of two alleles (different forms of a gene) coming from the parents.

3 **Pollination** is the process of sexual reproduction in a plant, where the pollen is transferred from the anther to the stigma of the flower.

4 **Mutation** is a change in genetic material on a chromosome.

Questions 28 through 32

Food webs are diagrams that indicate the flow of energy through an ecosystem. The arrows in a food web diagram indicate the direction of the flow—from eaten to eater, from prey to predator.

28. *The green plant is a producer.*

    Producers are organisms which make their own food, using the Sun's energy. Plants do this through the process of photosynthesis.

29. *The grasshopper is a herbivore. (So is the mouse, when it eats a plant—but a better answer for the mouse is in question 31.)*

    Herbivores are organisms that eat plants.

30. *The owl, the snake, and the frog are all carnivores. (So is the mouse, when it eats a grasshopper—but a better answer for the mouse is in question 31.)*

    Carnivores are organisms that eat animals.

31. *The mouse is an omnivore.*

    Omnivores are organisms that eat plants and animals

32. *The frog and mouse populations would increase and they would eat more grasshoppers.*

    If snakes were removed, there would be more frogs and mice, since the snakes would not be there to eat the frogs and mice. And if there were more frogs and mice, they would eat more grasshoppers—and the grasshopper population would decrease.

33. *The diagram shows asexual reproduction.*

    Asexual reproduction has a single parent. The process of duplicating the genetic material and splitting the cell is called mitosis. Mitosis and binary fission (splitting into two cells), and cell division are also acceptable answers.

34. *The genetic material in the two is the same.*

    In asexual reproduction, the genetic material of the offspring (daughter cell) is an exact copy of the genetic material of the parent.

Part C

35. *The student could use the magnet to attract the iron from the mixture.*

This is because a mixture is made of substances that still keep their own characteristics. According to the charts shown, after a physical change the iron is still magnetic and, therefore, could be attracted by the magnet.

36. *A compound was formed with different properties from those of the separate elements.*

A chemical change results in a compound with different characteristics that cannot be transformed back into the original elements. The chart for iron sulfide indicates that it no longer has the magnetic properties of the iron nor the color of either the iron or the sulfur.

37. *Chemical energy is converted to heat energy.*

You could give either answer to this question. As the wax is burned, it combines with oxygen in the air to produce water vapor, carbon dioxide, and carbon particles (soot). This process releases some of the chemical energy binding together the molecules of the wax. The transformation produces both heat energy and light energy.

38. *Mechanical energy is converted to sound energy.*

As the bell is rung, mechanical energy from muscles is transferred to the bell's clapper, making sound energy as it hits the side of the bell. To go back a little further, chemical energy stored in the muscles is converted to the mechanical energy that rings the bell.

39. *Hypothesis:* The height of the ball's bounce depends on the hardness of the court surface. (Or, the ball will bounce higher on a harder surface.)

Factor to be varied: Hardness of the surface of the court

Two factors to be held constant: ball, drop height, environmental temperature. Other answers, such as environmental temperature, are possible—but using the same ball and keeping the drop height constant are the most important.

Examples of procedures:

- Drop a tennis ball from a 6-foot height onto a tennis court and measure how high the ball bounces. Do the exact same thing on other courts of different surfaces. Repeat this procedure several times. Compare the results.
- Attach a meter stick to a wall and bounce a tennis ball near it. Record how high the ball bounces. Do the same thing on different surfaces. Compare the results.

- Using several courts with different surfaces, set up a meter stick and bounce a ball next to it. Drop the ball from exactly the same height each time. Record how high the ball bounces. Do this test several times.

Another name for scientific experiments is **scientific inquiry**. In order to explore natural phenomena, people need to formulate questions, set up a fair test which is a model of the phenomena they want to study, use appropriate tools to collect and record data, and evaluate the original hypothesis in light of the data.

In this example, the student noticed that the tennis ball bounced at different heights depending on the surface of the court. She developed a question to investigate, came up with a hypothesis, decided what factor she would vary, and kept other factors constant or the same so that she would be conducting a fair test.

The student developed a procedure to test her hypothesis and planned to perform the test several times to increase the chances of having accurate data.

Although the sample test did not ask for it, the experiment would continue with the student collecting and interpreting the data. She could have shared her data with her friends and asked for their opinions. She might have developed a graphic presentation of the data. She might have decided to adjust her inquiry based on her discussions.

Finally, she may have written her hypothesis and procedures down so that other people interested in the same question could duplicate her study.

40. *The graph should look like the following:*

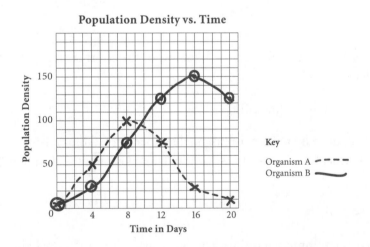

It is important in science to accurately represent data in a variety of ways. In this experiment showing the comparison of growth in organisms A and B the data can be shown both in chart form, as in the original data table, and on a graph. Notice, however, how much easier it is to see a pattern when you look at a graph than when you look at the original data table.

41. *Several answers might explain the decline in Organism A's population when grown in the same test tube as Organism B:*

- **Competition** – Organism A might not have been as successful as Organism B in competing for resources.
- **Toxin** – Organism B may have given off some toxin or substance poisonous to Organism A.
- **Predator-prey relationship** – Organism B may have eaten Organism A.

42. *Continuing the lines on the graph gives the following approximate results for population density at day 21:*

- *Organism A – 5*
- *Organism B – 115*

The populations of both organisms peaked (Organism A on day 8 and Organism B on day 16). Since then, their populations have steadily declined. A continued decrease in population density could be expected on day 21.

One possible reason for the continuing decline in both populations is that most of the available nutrients in the test tube have been consumed. Another possible reason is that the organisms are being poisoned by their wastes, which are not being removed from the system.

43. *The track of the hailstone should look something like this:*

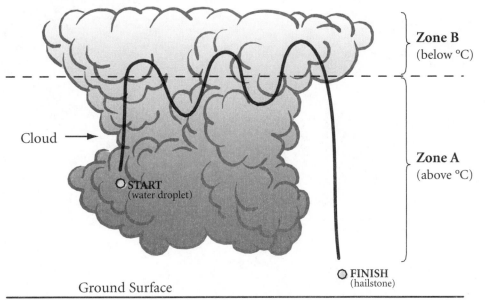

The hailstone had 3 layers. This means that the track of the hailstone you drew should have gone from the Start point up into Zone B, where the temperature is below freezing (below 0° Celsius), three times. As the Background Information points out, a layer is formed on a hailstone each time it moves back into an area where ice would be formed.

44.   *The hailstorm on August 12 probably had the strongest updrafts.*

On August 12, the diameter of the hailstones reached 20 mm. In order to reach this size the updrafts needed to be strong enough to lift the stones into Zone B, the freezing zone. Also, as each layer of ice was added, the stones would become heavier. So very strong winds would be needed to push the hailstones back up into the air.

45.   *Hailstorms can cause all of the following problems: damage to crops, buildings, and/or vehicles.*

To find examples of a problem caused by hailstorms, simply reread the page of the student's notes where the "Background Information Found in Science Book" is listed.

A good test-taking strategy is to carefully read the question. Item number 45 is a good example. It tells you exactly where to find the information you need.

NEW YORK STATE INTERMEDIATE LEVEL SCIENCE
Practice Test 2

Part A

1   Many of the chemical reactions that take place in a cell occur in the watery material lying between the nucleus and the cell membrane. This material is called

   1 cytoplasm
   2 chloroplast
   3 cell wall
   4 blood plasma

2   Which human body system regulates the disposal of solid, liquid, and gaseous waste molecules?

   1 skeletal
   2 endocrine
   3 respiratory
   4 excretory

3   The chlorophyll necessary for photosynthesis is found in a cell's

   1 chromosomes
   2 cytoplasm
   3 chloroplasts
   4 membranes

4   Selective breeding and genetic engineering may contribute to

   1 extinction
   2 variations in species
   3 metamorphosis
   4 increased disease

5   The scientific name for the wolf is *Canis lupus*. Which classification group does the word *Canis* refer to?

   1 kingdom
   2 phylum
   3 genus
   4 species

6   What life process is shown in the diagram below?

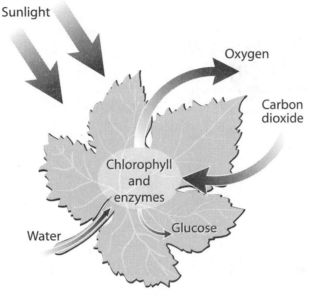

1 circulation
2 photosynthesis
3 natural selection
4 transformation

7   In a swamp ecosystem, the heron and the snapping turtle both eat the same species of minnow.
     These feeding patterns will most likely result in

     1 the destruction of the plants in the swamp
     2 competition between the heron and the turtle
     3 extinction of the heron
     4 rapid evolution of a new fish species

8   The liquid part of Earth's surface is called the

     1 hydrosphere
     2 lithosphere
     3 troposphere
     4 atmosphere

9   What conditions during the rock cycle cause solid rocks to become liquid?

     1 sedimentation and erosion
     2 high temperatures and pressure
     3 magma breaking and cooling
     4 absorption and crystallization

10   According to the diagram, what phase of the moon would an observer on Earth see?

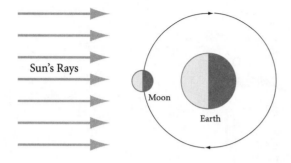

   1 new
   2 crescent
   3 quarter
   4 full

11   The Sun appears to rise along the eastern horizon and set along the western horizon because of

   1 Earth's rotation
   2 Earth's revolution
   3 Sun's rotation
   4 Sun's revolution

12   In which situation is a physical reaction occurring?

   1 a nail rusts
   2 a log burns
   3 sugar dissolves in water
   4 an egg is cooked in boiling water

13   As butter melts, its molecules

   1 absorb heat energy and move farther apart
   2 absorb heat energy and move closer together
   3 release heat energy and move farther apart
   4 release heat energy and move closer together

14   Skiers are pulled uphill by a moving rope at the ski slope. When they reach the top of the hill, they ski down. What type of energy do the skiers gain as they move uphill?

   1 mechanical
   2 heat
   3 kinetic
   4 potential

15 Which diagram shows the best way to increase the solubility of the sugar cube?

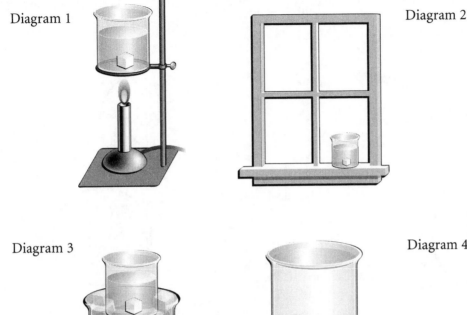

Diagram 1

Diagram 2

Diagram 3

Diagram 4

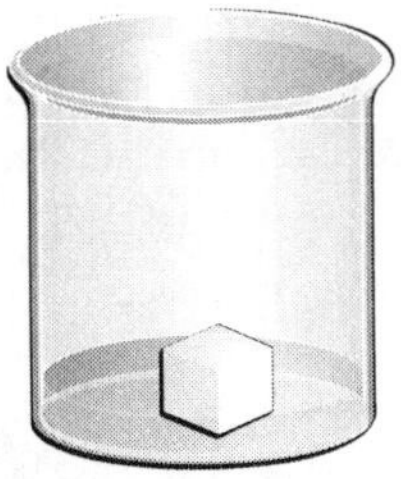

1 Diagram 1
2 Diagram 2
3 Diagram 3
4 Diagram 4

16 What form of energy is produced when a telephone rings?

1 mechanical
2 electrical
3 chemical
4 sound

17 Which of the following uses lenses to bend light and make objects that are far away seem much closer?

1 microscope
2 microwave
3 television
4 telescope

Part B

18. Which statement below best explains the key part of the carbon-oxygen cycle shown in the diagram?

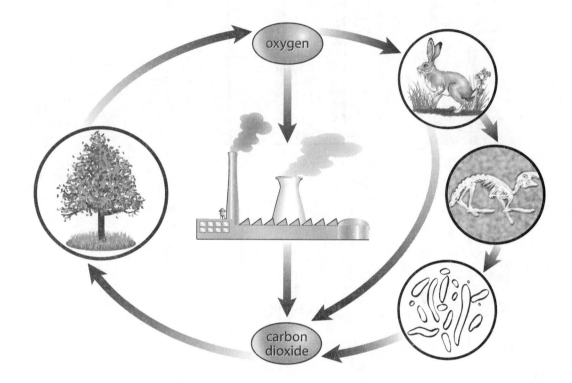

1 decomposers add oxygen to the atmosphere and remove carbon dioxide
2 burning fuel adds oxygen to the atmosphere and removes carbon dioxide
3 producers give off oxygen and use carbon dioxide
4 consumers give off oxygen and use carbon dioxide

19. Use the picture below to help answer the question. In this ecosystem there are many organisms and many relationships. For each of the relationships listed below, name the two organisms and describe their interaction.

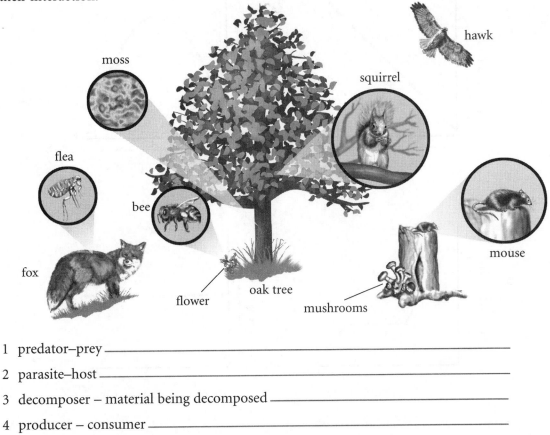

1 predator–prey _____

2 parasite–host _____

3 decomposer – material being decomposed _____

4 producer – consumer _____

20. What is the length of the snail shown in the diagram?

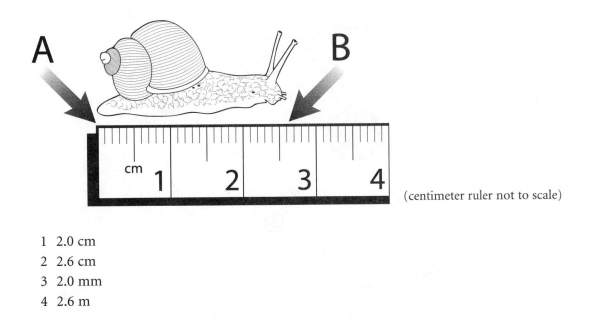

(centimeter ruler not to scale)

1 2.0 cm

2 2.6 cm

3 2.0 mm

4 2.6 m

21. Chemical reactions are affected by temperature. Which graph below best shows the relationship between temperature and rate of reaction?

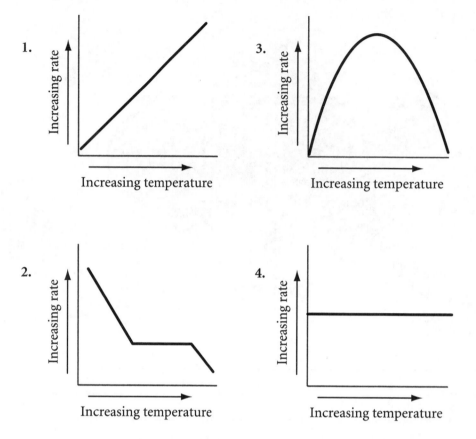

22. On the diagram below mark an "X" to show where the Earth will be in six months.

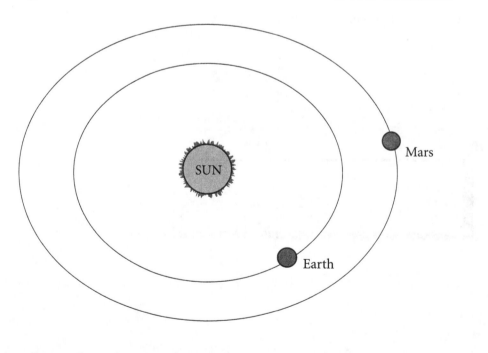

23. On the diagram at the bottom of p. 144, draw and label the approximate orbits of Mercury and Venus.

24. How much time does it take for the Earth to spin once on its axis?

    1 one year
    2 one month
    3 one day
    4 one hour

25. What keeps the Earth in orbit around the Sun?

    1 solar power
    2 wind
    3 jet stream
    4 gravity

26. Mars is a planet, not a star. It gives off no light of its own. Yet a person standing on Earth is able to see Mars shining in the night sky. Explain how this is possible.

    _____
    _____
    _____
    _____
    _____

27. A student recorded the following observations about two rock samples:

Characteristics	Rock A	Rock B
color	some black crystals, some white crystals	white crystals with some brown streaks
size of crystal	large	small

    What evidence shown in the table suggests that Rock A is made of more than one mineral?

    _____
    _____
    _____
    _____

28. What evidence suggests that Rock B in Question 27 cooled quickly?

_____

_____

_____

_____

29. The metamorphic rock known as marble forms from the sedimentary rock limestone. What actions must have taken place to change the limestone to marble?

_____

_____

_____

_____

30. The diagram below shows an experimental set up to determine how plants lose water.

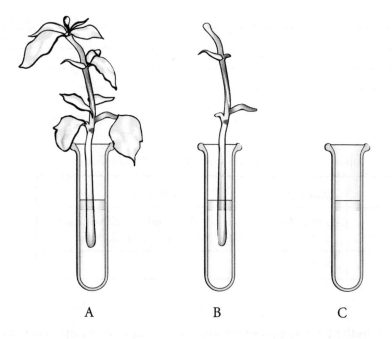

A   B   C

The test tubes were massed at the beginning of the experiment and the following day.
The results are shown in the following table.

Test Tube	mass of tube and contents on Day 1	mass of tube and contents on Day 2
A	33.0 g	29.5 g
B	28.0 g	27.5 g
C	26.0 g	26.0 g

Which tube lost the most mass?

_____

31. Explain why this tube lost the most.

_____
_____
_____
_____

32. What function does Tube C serve?

_____
_____
_____
_____

33. In a certain species of plant, the gene for red flowers (R) was dominant over the gene for white flowers (r). Pure red flowers were crossed with white flowers. The Punnett square below shows the results of the cross.

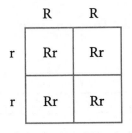

What percentage of plants would have white flowers?

_____

34. If two of these offspring were crossed, what color flowers would result? Use a Punnett square to show your answer.

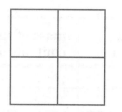

35. Genes are composed of DNA. In what structures of the cell can they be found?

    1 cell membrane
    2 cell wall
    3 chromosomes
    4 cytoplasm

Part C

Carbon dioxide is necessary for life on earth. In spite of its importance, environmentalists worldwide are concerned about emissions of carbon dioxide and other gases from coal burning factories.

36. Identify one harmful effect of increased levels of carbon dioxide in the atmosphere.

    _____

    _____

    _____

    _____

37. Explain how the increased level of carbon dioxide causes this effect.

    _____

    _____

    _____

    _____

38. Increased levels of sulfur dioxide in the atmosphere are another result of factory emissions. New York State lakes have shown the effects of these higher amounts of sulfur dioxide.

    Identify the harmful compound formed from these emissions, including how it is formed.

    _____
    _____
    _____
    _____

39. Explain the resulting condition of the lakes and the effects on wildlife in the area.

    _____
    _____
    _____
    _____

Read the following informational selection. Then answer questions 40–42, which are based on the information in the selection.

> Boston is one of the oldest and largest metropolitan areas in the United States, covering more than 1,500 square kilometers. In 1889 the Metropolitan Sewerage Board was established to deal with the growing pollution of Boston's rivers and harbor. More than a century later, pollution is still a problem. Now, in addition to the continued sewage problem, heavy metals such as chromium, copper, lead, and zinc contaminate the sediments in the harbor as well as the fish and shellfish.
>
> The United States Geological Survey is conducting studies of Boston Harbor, determining levels of contaminants, and estimating rates of sediment accumulation. They have discovered that the islands surrounding the harbor block ocean currents that would help disperse urban pollution.

40. Years ago, managers of industries thought dumping chemical waste products into rivers would be an efficient way of disposing of them. Identify two environmentally sound ways that industries currently use to take care of by-products of manufacturing processes.

    _____
    _____
    _____
    _____
    _____

41. Heavy metals are dangerous to fish and shellfish. Explain how the levels of these toxic chemicals change in the birds that eat the fish.

    _____
    _____
    _____
    _____
    _____
    _____

42. Using the data they collected, the U.S. Geological Survey along with the Massachusetts Water Resources Authority designed a procedure to collect and dump the contaminants farther out into the ocean. Explain why this solution is less harmful than letting the sediments remain in the harbor.

    _____
    _____
    _____
    _____
    _____

Read the following informational paragraph. Then answer questions 43–45, which are based upon the paragraph.

In folktales, wolves are big, bad, and ugly! Actually, wolves aren't all that big, and they're certainly not all bad. Humans nearly eliminated wolves in the United States in the 1930's by putting bounties on them. Officials found out, almost too late, that wolves play a very important part in the ecosystem. They only eat about three-quarters of the animals they kill, leaving the rest for other scavengers like foxes and coyotes. When coyotes don't find enough to eat they turn to small mammals, like rabbits and mice, for their food. With fewer small mammals to eat the grasses, the plants begin to crowd each other and do not flourish. Humans hunt elk, but they don't usually kill enough to thin an elk herd. The excess elk starve to death without wolves to keep them in check.

43. Based on the information in the passage, draw a food web to show the relationship between the organisms mentioned.

44. Choose three organisms from the paragraph above and identify their roles in the ecosystem.

_____

_____

_____

_____

_____

_____

_____

_____

45. Wolves hunt in packs. Describe how the process of natural selection might take place in a pack of wolves.

_____

_____

_____

_____

_____

_____

_____

_____

NEW YORK STATE INTERMEDIATE LEVEL SCIENCE
Part D—Performance Test

An important part of scientific inquiry is asking questions, using materials and recording and analyzing the data collected. The performance tasks in Part D of the *Intermediate-Level Science Test* give you an opportunity to use these skills and apply your knowledge of science content.

When you actually perform these tasks, or tasks similar to those given here, during your examination period, you will have 15 minutes per task to do the work and answer the questions. Although you will not be performing the tasks here, study the diagram of how the materials will be set up, and read through the directions outlining what you will be asked to do.

1. Experimenting with a Ball and Ramp

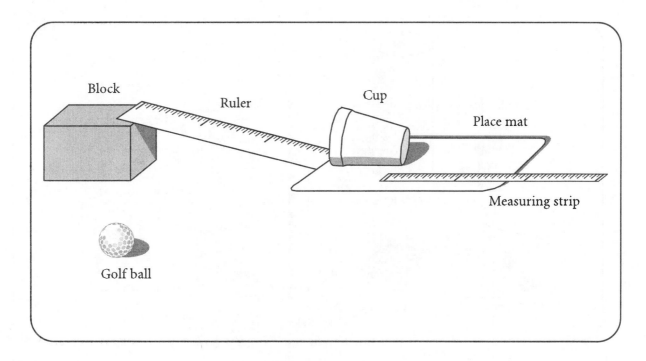

For this task you will be asked to observe a golf ball rolling down a ramp (ruler) and moving a plastic cup. You will identify some variables that would affect how far the cup moves.

In the first part of this activity the cup to be moved always has the same mass (16.0 grams). The distance pushed depends on where the ball is released on the ramp. You will record the data for 5 trials. After analyzing the data you collected during the first part of the activity, you will be asked to design a study to determine how changing the mass of the cup will change the distance it is moved by the golf ball.

You will be directed to write your recommendations about where the release point for the ball should be for each new trial and, finally, to write a hypothesis about the distance the cups of different masses will be moved by the golf ball.

As you complete your trials and analyze your data to help you design the next experiment you should remember to:

- follow all directions
- complete all the trials
- neatly and accurately complete your data table
- change only one variable at a time
- relate the mass of the cup to the distance moved

2. Soaps and Water

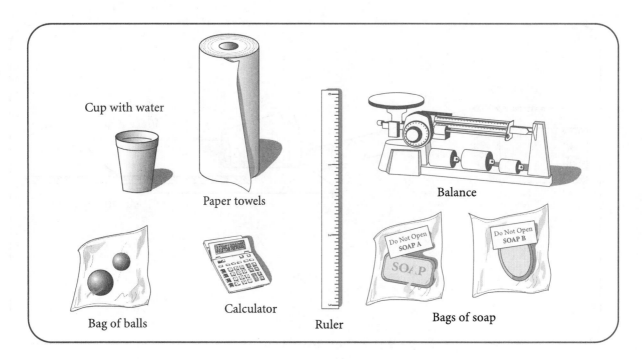

For this task you will be asked to determine the properties of two soap samples and predict how they will behave when placed in water. You will place the samples in water and compare their densities.

You will be given two soap samples in plastic bags and asked to measure and record the mass, length, width, and height of each sample. You will use the formula for density to determine the density of one sample and the volume of the other. Since predicting is an important part of scientific inquiry, you will be asked to use your data to predict the position of the samples of soap if they were placed in a container of water. Finally, using a rubber ball and a Styrofoam ball, you will observe the position of each ball in a cup of water and make some observations about their densities.

As you answer the questions and complete the data tables for this task, remember to:

- carefully measure the mass and dimensions of the samples
- show your work as you do your calculations of density and volume
- use the observations you made of the soap samples to help you compare the densities of the two types of balls
- remember the definition of density: mass per unit volume, or $\frac{\text{mass}}{\text{volume}}$. If the density is less than 1, the object floats; if greater than 1, it sinks.

3   Cell Size

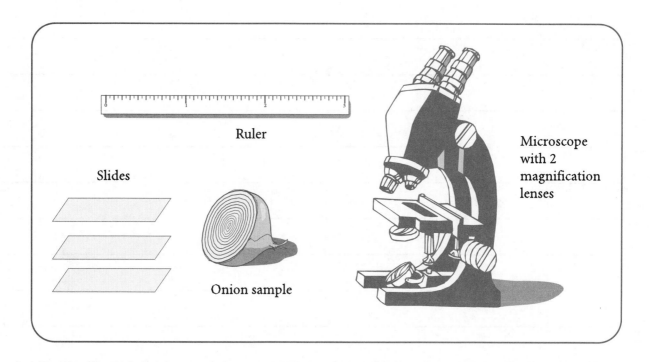

Ruler

Slides

Onion sample

Microscope
with 2
magnification
lenses

For this task you will measure the size of a microscope's field of view, estimate the size of a cell, and draw pictures of the cells as you observe them under the microscope.

You will be asked to measure the microscope's field of view by looking at a slide of graph paper under the microscope. Once you have determined the diameter of the lowest power's field of view, you will look at a slide of an onion skin, sketch what you see, and determine the length of one cell in your diagram. Finally, you will look at a last slide under high power, and draw the shape and structure of the cells you observe.

As you do your calculations and sketch the cells remember to:

*   accurately count the grids of the graph paper
*   sketch the onion cells neatly, in a continuous row across the field of view
*   carefully divide the microscope's field of view by the number of cells to find the length of one cell
*   carefully and completely sketch one cell from the field of view under high power

Notes

Notes

Notes